Advisory Group on Non-ionising Radiation

CHAIRMAN

Sir Richard Doll
Imperial Cancer Research Fund Cancer Studies Unit, Oxford

MEMBERS

Dr V Beral
Director, Cancer Epidemiology Unit, Imperial Cancer Research Fund, Oxford
Dr R Cox
National Radiological Protection Board, Chilton
Professor N E Day
Director, Biostatistics Unit, Medical Research Council, Cambridge
Professor M J Gardner
Medical Research Council, Environmental Epidemiology Unit, Southampton
Professor E H Grant
Physics Department, King's College, London
Dr A F McKinlay
National Radiological Protection Board, Chilton
Dr C R Muirhead
National Radiological Protection Board, Chilton
Dr R D Saunders
National Radiological Protection Board, Chilton
Dr J W Stather
National Radiological Protection Board, Chilton

OBSERVERS

Dr H Williams
Department of Health, London
Dr B H MacGibbon
National Radiological Protection Board, Chilton

CONSULTANTS

Mr S G Allen
National Radiological Protection Board, Leeds
Dr J A Dennis
Formerly Assistant Director (Physical Sciences),
National Radiological Protection Board, Chilton

1 Introduction

1   The levels of electric and magnetic fields to which people may be exposed were, until the beginning of this century, extremely low. Modern industrial development has resulted in increasing levels of exposure of people to a complex mix of artificially elevated electromagnetic fields that span a very wide frequency range. One of the most significant contributions to this changing environment has been the technological advances associated with the growth of electrical power generation and transmission systems and their use in domestic and occupational situations. In addition, electromagnetic field generating devices have proliferated in telecommunications and broadcasting, in industrial plants, office buildings, public transportation systems, homes, cars and elsewhere.

2   Until recently, the assessment of potential exposure was primarily based on environmental field measurements at positions that people might occupy. Whilst useful for comparison with derived reference field strength levels contained in protection guidelines, such information is of limited value when assessing the actual exposure of people over time and space. This is particularly so close to sources, where fields are complex, and where absorbed energy or the distribution of induced currents in the body may be difficult to evaluate. Better understanding of the way in which electromagnetic fields interact with the human body, and the development of techniques to assess quantities relevant to personal exposure, is improving exposure assessment. At the frequencies used for power distribution, the development of new personal monitoring equipment with data logging capabilities is providing better information on the time distribution of exposure, if this is indeed important in relation to any risk.

3   The National Radiological Protection Board has the responsibility for advising UK government departments on standards of protection for exposure to non-ionising radiation. This responsibility covers static and low frequency electric and magnetic fields and radiofrequency (including microwave) radiations, as well as optical radiation. The electromagnetic spectrum is shown in Table 2.1 (p 5), which also gives the main sources of exposure in the different frequency bands. Electric and magnetic fields are generated both deliberately and adventitiously. The nature of these fields in the home and workplace, the potential influence of changing practices, and practical aspects of field strength measurements are described in Chapter 2.

4   Many of the biological effects of exposure to electromagnetic fields are well understood and consistent with established mechanisms of physical interaction with tissues. These include perception processes associated with the accumulation and redistribution of electric charge on the surface of the body, effects on electrically excitable tissue such as nerves and muscles, and effects caused by heating of tissues. Experimental and epidemiological studies on the biological effects of exposure to non-ionising radiations have recently been reviewed in a series of publications by the Board[1-4].

5   To a large measure the extent of acute effects on the human body and their

dependence on the frequency and magnitude of the fields can be predicted from existing knowledge of their effects on humans[3], from experimental studies in animals[4], and by the application of modelling studies that predict the efficiency with which animals and humans interact with incident fields. These sources of information, together with the application of appropriate safety margins, have formed the basis of national and international exposure guidelines[5-11]. Apart from medical exposures, only a relatively small number of people are likely to be exposed to fields at levels large enough to result in acute effects.

6   There have been suggestions that other effects may occur at much lower levels of exposure. The most important of these is cancer but other possible effects, including modifications to melatonin production, changes in ion fluxes across cell membranes, and changes in the rate of cell division and transformation, have also been reported[1-4]. Although experimental studies have shown that electromagnetic fields can, in some circumstances, affect the physiology and biochemistry of cells, they do not appear to damage directly the genetic material, DNA, in cells and therefore are unlikely to act as an initiator of cancer. Experimental studies on the effects of electromagnetic fields on cellular and animal systems are discussed in Chapter 3.

7   Cancer was first associated epidemiologically with exposure to electromagnetic fields in 1979 when Wertheimer and Leeper[12] reported that the proportion of children dying from cancer that resided in homes adjacent to high current configuration power lines, used as a surrogate for electromagnetic field exposure, was greater than the proportion of other children selected to be representative of the population as a whole. Many other studies have been reported relating the risk of cancer to domestic exposure, to sources of electromagnetic fields, to parental exposure or to employment in occupations where exposure to such fields might be considered to be unusually high[4, 13-16]. The results have, however, been difficult to interpret and these studies are therefore examined in detail in Chapters 4–7.

8   Recently reported epidemiological studies and laboratory research have raised questions about the adequacy of the existing guidelines for limiting exposure to electromagnetic fields. These have to take into account the balance of benefits and risks. The benefits associated with the sources of the fields are, however, clear, while the magnitude of the risks associated with low level exposures, if indeed there are any such risks, is certainly not. If, therefore, it is only sensible at the moment to retain the present guidelines, which are based on known and quantifiable effects, it is essential that the results of the recent studies on low level effects are kept under constant review, to ensure that the guidelines are based on the best available information. Many of these studies were reviewed in a draft document issued by the American Environmental Protection Agency (EPA) on an 'Evaluation of the Potential Carcinogenicity of Electromagnetic Fields'. This report has not yet been formally published but has received considerable attention. Following the issue of the EPA draft report, the Director of the Board set up an Advisory Group on Non-ionising Radiation which has as its terms of reference a remit.

'to review work on the biological effects of non-ionising radiation relevant to human health and to advise on research priorities'

9   The first objective of the Advisory Group has been to review epidemiological and laboratory studies relevant to the possible carcinogenic effect of electromagnetic fields and to determine the extent to which the weight of evidence suggests they should be treated as a potential carcinogen. The emphasis of the present work has been on exposure to time varying fields. The Advisory Group has also made recommendations about further studies that need to be undertaken in the field of epidemiology and some preliminary recommendations about further experimental studies. The Advisory Group wishes to acknowledge the help of Mr S G Allen who helped in the preparation of Chapter 2.

REFERENCES

1   Kowalczuk, C I, Sienkiewicz, Z J, and Saunders, R D. Biological effects of exposure to non-ionising electromagnetic fields and radiation: I. Static electric and magnetic fields. Chilton, NRPB-R238 (1991) (London, HMSO).

2   Sienkiewicz, Z J, Saunders, R D, and Kowalczuk, C I. Biological effects of exposure to non-ionising electromagnetic fields and radiation: II. Extremely low frequency electric and magnetic fields. Chilton, NRPB-R239 (1991) (London, HMSO).

3   Saunders, R D, Kowalczuk, C I, and Sienkiewicz, Z J. Biological effects of exposure to non-ionising electromagnetic fields and radiation: III. Radiofrequency and microwave radiation. Chilton, NRPB-R240 (1991) (London, HMSO).

4   Dennis, J A, Muirhead, C R, and Ennis, J R. Human health and exposure to electromagnetic radiation. Chilton, NRPB-R241 (1992) (London, HMSO).

5   ANSI. Safety levels with respect to human exposure to radiofrequency electromagnetic fields, 300 kHz to 100 GHz. New York, Institute of Electrical and Electronic Engineers, American National Standard C95.1 (1982).

6   WHO. Radiofrequency and microwaves. Geneva, World Health Organisation, Environmental Health Criteria 16 (1981).

7   WHO. Extremely low frequency (ELF) fields. Geneva, World Health Organisation, Environmental Health Criteria 35 (1984).

8   WHO. Magnetic fields. Geneva, World Health Organisation, Environmental Health Criteria 69 (1987).

9   IRPA. Interim guidelines on limits of exposure to radiofrequency electromagnetic fields in the frequency range 100 kHz to 300 GHz. *Health Phys.*, **46**, 975 (1984).

10 IRPA. Guidelines on limits of exposure to radiofrequency electromagnetic fields in the frequency range 100 kHz to 300 GHz. *Health Phys.*, **54**, 115 (1988).

11 NRPB. Guidance as to restrictions on exposures to time varying electromagnetic fields and the 1988 recommendations of the International Non-ionizing Radiation Committee. Chilton, NRPB-GS11 (1989) (London, HMSO).

12 Wertheimer, N, and Leeper, E. Electrical wiring configurations and childhood cancer. *Am. J. Epidemiol.*, **109**, 273 (1979).

13 Dennis, J A, Muirhead, C R, and Ennis, J R. Epidemiological studies of exposure to electromagnetic fields. II. Cancer. *J. Radiol. Prot.*, **11**, 13 (1991).

14 Sheikh, K. Exposure to electromagnetic fields and the risk of cancer. *Arch. Environ. Health*, **41**, 1 (1988).

15 Coleman, M P, and Beral, V. A review of epidemiological studies of health effects of living near or working with electricity generation and transmission equipment. *Int. J. Epidemiol.*, **17**, 1 (1988).

16 Repacholi, M H. Carcinogenic potential of extremely low frequency fields. IN *Non-ionising Radiation* (M H Repacholi, ed). London, Institute of Nuclear Engineers, p 303 (1988).

2 Electromagnetic Field Exposure at Home and in the Workplace

INTRODUCTION

1   Today, everyone is exposed to electric and magnetic fields arising from a wide variety of sources which use electrical energy both at home and at work. The fields which are of interest here are time varying fields with frequencies of up to 300 gigahertz (GHz) or 300 000 million cycles per second. These fields lie within that part of the electromagnetic spectrum bounded by static fields and infrared radiation. At the highest frequency of 300 GHz there is insufficient quantum energy to cause ionisation in matter, consequently this region of the spectrum, together with optical frequencies, is referred to as non-ionising. Whilst the term radiation might be appropriate at high frequencies, it is preferable to think in terms of the individual electric and magnetic field components at frequencies where there is only a slow variation with time such as 50/60 Hz used for power generation and distribution.

2   The International Telecommunications Union (ITU) has divided the spectrum to 300 GHz into bands. Within this frequency range, the nature of the exposure fields and their characteristics can vary greatly, corresponding to the wide variety of sources and applications[1,2]. Some of the sources of electromagnetic field exposure and their approximate position within the ITU band designation are shown in Table 2.1, together with frequency and wavelength correspondence for the band divisions. The term radiofrequency (RF) tends to be arbitrarily defined to cover various bands of the spectrum, sometimes restricted to frequencies below 300 MHz but also used to embrace the bands above 300 MHz defined as microwaves. In the same way that RF and microwaves are used as descriptive rather than definitive terms, ELF is also used generically to include all frequencies between static fields and 3 kHz. This broad description of the electromagnetic spectrum is illustrated in Figure 2.1.

3   Unlike ionising radiation where natural sources contribute the greater proportion of the exposure to the population, man-made sources tend to dominate exposure to time varying fields and radiation. Over parts of the frequency spectrum such as those used for electrical power and broadcasting, man-made fields are many thousands of times greater than natural fields arising from either the sun or the earth. For example, the power flux density of radiation emitted by the earth at a surface temperature of 20 °C is about one-million times smaller than the median exposure of city dwellers in the USA from radio and television transmissions over the 1 MHz to 1 GHz frequency range.

4   Static fields are not specifically addressed in this report; however, the natural fields to which people are unavoidably exposed are the earth's static fields. Everyone is exposed to the static magnetic field arising from current flow in the earth's core. This gives rise to a magnetic flux density of 30–70 microteslas (μT) over the surface of the planet dependent on location. Some people may be exposed to magnetic fields exceeding 1 tesla (T) when close to magnets used for medical

Frequency	Wavelength	Description	Band	Sources
0 Hz		Static		Earth's field Magnets, DC supplies
		Sub-extremely low frequency	SELF	
30 Hz	10 000 km			Electric power lines and cables. Domestic and industrial appliances
50 Hz	6 000 km	Extremely low frequency	ELF	
300 Hz	1 000 km			
		Voice frequency*	VF	Induction heaters
3 kHz	100 km			
		Very low frequency	VLF	Television sets Visual display units
30 kHz	10 km			
		Low frequency	LF	AM radio
300 kHz	1 km			
		Medium frequency	MF	Induction heaters
3 MHz	100 m			
		High frequency	HF	RF heat sealers
30 MHz	10 m			
		Very high frequency	VHF	FM radio
300 MHz	1 m			
		Ultra high frequency	UHF	Cellular telephones Television broadcast Microwave ovens
3 GHz	10 cm			
		Super high frequency	SHF	Radar Satellite links Microwave communications
30 GHz	1 cm			
		Extra high frequency	EHF	Point-to-point links
300 GHz	1 mm			
		Infrared		

TABLE 2.1
Electromagnetic fields and their sources

*Radiofrequencies equivalent to speech (sound) frequencies.
Note 1000 Hz = 1 kHz; 1000 kHz = 1 MHz; 1000 MHz = 1 GHz.

FIGURE 2.1 *Electromagnetic spectrum*

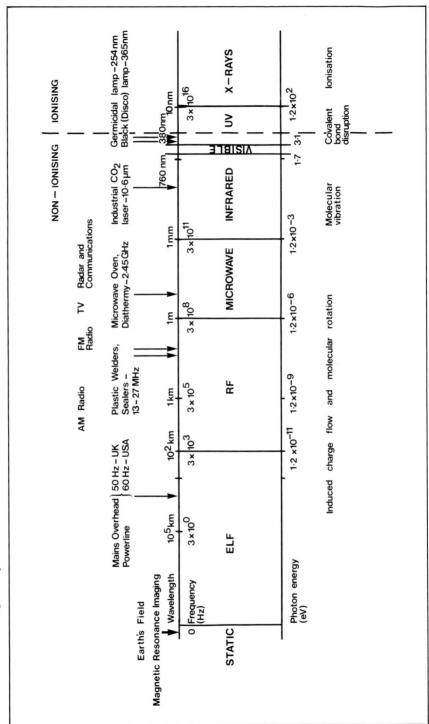

6

and research purposes (eg magnetic resonance imaging, particle accelerators and fusion reactors).

5   The earth's static electric field strength changes with weather conditions and in quiescent periods is 100–200 volts per metre (V m^{-1}) whilst in stormy conditions can be tens of thousands of volts per metre. Electrostatic fields of several thousand volts per metre can be encountered from charged objects in the home and at work.

6   Naturally occurring time varying magnetic fields are associated with changes in ionospheric currents which are most affected by the sun's activity. Magnetic flux densities of 0.5 μT at frequencies of a few Hz can be generated at times of intense solar activity, but normal daily variations from pulses of less than 0.1 Hz are about 0.03 μT. Lightning strikes can generate a wide range of frequencies up to the MHz region, the peak intensity occurring at a few kHz, but under normal circumstances the magnetic flux density decreases from 10^{-5} μT at several Hz to 10^{-8} μT at a few kHz. Atmospheric time varying electric fields up to 1 kHz are less than 0.5 V m^{-1} and decrease with increasing frequency.

7   The most common man-made time varying fields to which people are continually exposed are those arising from the use of 50/60 Hz electrical power transmission and distribution, the use of electrical appliances and various radio and TV transmitters. Everywhere that TV or radio signals are received there must be an RF field; low level exposure is ubiquitous. The general public is also exposed to low level fields from microwave communications links, radar, and domestic products such as microwave ovens, TVs and computer displays (VDUs). Higher exposures can arise transiently in close proximity to sources such as citizens' band (CB) or mobile and portable radio antennas.

8   The potential for people to be exposed depends not only on the strength of the electromagnetic fields generated but also on their distance from the source and, in the case of a directional antenna such as radar, their proximity to the main beam. High power broadcast and highly directional radar systems do not necessarily present a source of material exposure except to specialist maintenance workers or engineers. Millions of people, however, come in close proximity to low power RF transmitters and electrical appliances where field strengths, intense at close distances, can give rise to non-uniform, partial body exposure. The field strengths decrease rapidly with distance from a particular source.

9   Over recent decades the use of electrical energy has increased substantially, both for power at mains supply frequencies and for RF broadcast and telecommunications purposes. At RF frequencies used for broadcast, it is clear that exposure of the population will have increased in proportion with increasing power. The proliferation of mobile and portable sources for telecommunications will have increased the exposure of people using such equipment. It is clear also that the introduction of more electrical appliances into the home will have increased exposure to 50/60 Hz fields. The manner in which exposure to fields from local electricity distribution reflects the increased power utilisation is less clear, as the magnetic fields are a complex function of currents flowing in cables, wires and pipes and depend on wiring and earthing practices which may have changed with time.

NON-IONISING FIELDS AND RADIATION

General properties

10   The quantities and units described in this report are summarised in Table 2.2.

11   The frequency and wavelength of electromagnetic radiation are related by the velocity in the medium through which the radiation travels; in air the velocity is about 300-million metres per second (3×10^8 m s^{-1}). The relationship between frequency (f), wavelength (λ), and velocity (c) is given by $c = f\lambda$.

12   When electromagnetic radiation travels through biological tissue the wavelength shortens depending on the electrical properties of the tissue in question. In their simplest form the waves are sinusoidal, the magnitude of the electric and magnetic fields increasing and decreasing together with time. The electric and magnetic fields are at right angles to one another and to the direction of propagation of the energy. The unit of electric field strength (E) is volt per metre (V m^{-1}); the unit of magnetic field strength (H) is ampere per metre (A m^{-1}); and the unit of power density (S), which is the vector product of E and H, is watt per square metre (W m^{-2}). This latter quantity in the direction of the propagated energy is also referred to as the Poynting vector.

13   The magnetic flux density (B), which has the unit of tesla (T), will be used extensively in this report for consistency. The magnetic flux density is related to the magnetic field strength (H) by the magnetic permeability (μ) of the medium which is expressed in the unit of henry per metre (H m^{-1}):

$$B = \mu H$$

14   For most biological materials the permeability is the same value as μ_0, the permeability of free space, therefore there is a constant relationship between field strength measured in free space and flux density. Another, older unit of magnetic flux density which is often used in the literature is the gauss (G), where $1\,\text{T} = 10\,000\,\text{G}$. Tesla and its submultiples will be used throughout this report. Examples of the relationship between multiples and submultiples of the units are given in Table 2.3.

15   Whilst waveforms may be simple sinusoids, such as those used for 50 Hz power distribution, it is important to appreciate that in practice there is a wide variety of

TABLE 2.2
Quantities and units

Quantity	Symbol	Unit	Symbol
Current density	J	ampere per square metre	A m^{-2}
Conductivity	σ	siemen per metre	S m^{-1}
Electric field strength	E	volt per metre	V m^{-1}
Frequency	f	hertz	Hz
Magnetic field strength	H	ampere per metre	A m^{-1}
Magnetic flux density	B	tesla	T
Permeability	μ	henry per metre	H m^{-1}
Permittivity	ε	farad per metre	F m^{-1}
Power density	S	watt per square metre	W m^{-2}

Quantity and units	Equivalent multiples and submultiples
Frequency	
hertz (Hz)	1 GHz = 10^3 MHz = 10^6 kHz = 10^9 Hz
kilohertz (kHz)	1 MHz = 10^3 kHz = 10^6 Hz
megahertz (MHz)	1 kHz = 10^3 Hz
gigahertz (GHz)	
Electric field strength	
volt per metre (V m⁻¹)	1 kV m^{-1} = 10^3 V m^{-1}
kilovolt per metre (kV m⁻¹)	
Magnetic flux density	
tesla (T)	1 T = 10^3 mT = 10^6 μT = 10^9 nT
millitesla (mT)	1 mT = 10^3 μT = 10^6 nT
microtesla (μT)	1 μT = 10^3 nT
nanotesla (nT)	

modulations depending on the use of the frequency source. The waveform may be amplitude modulated (AM) or frequency modulated (FM) for radio communication, or pulse modulation can be used for systems such as radar where the microwave energy is carried in short bursts of around microsecond duration. In this latter case where the pulse width is usually short compared to the interval between pulses, the peak power can exceed the mean power by factors of 1000 or more. In the case of cathode ray tube displays, such as those used in TV and computer terminals, the requirement to deflect the electron beam to scan lines rapidly, results in a waveform which is sawtooth in appearance.

Near field and far field

16   The description of electromagnetic radiation given above where the electric and magnetic fields are in phase and are at right angles to the direction of propagation is known as far field or plane wave which describes the approximate nature of the wavefront at a distance of several wavelengths from a source. In these circumstances it is possible to relate *E*, *H* and *S* in a simple way. For waves in free space where the impedance is taken to be 377 Ω the relationship is

$$S = E^2/377 = 377H^2$$

17   Table 2.4 illustrates the far-field or plane-wave equivalent values of power density, electric field strength and magnetic field strength for power densities from 0.1 to 100 W m⁻². For comparison, the equivalent magnetic flux density is also given, the relative permeability (μ_r) of air and free space can be taken as $\mu_r = 1$. As the magnetic permeability of biological material is also similar to that of air, the presence of human beings does not materially affect magnetic fields measured in the absence of a person.

TABLE 2.4
Examples of
far-field
(plane-wave)
relationships

Power density (W m⁻²)	Electric field strength (V m⁻¹)	Magnetic field strength (A m⁻¹)	Equivalent magnetic flux density (μT)
0.1	6.14	0.016	0.020
1.0	19.42	0.052	0.065
10.0	61.40	0.163	0.204
50.0	137.30	0.364	0.455
100.0	194.16	0.515	0.644

18   It is important to make the distinction between *fields* and *radiation* to highlight that in some circumstances the electric and magnetic field components need to be assessed separately and that exposure may not always occur in the radiating far field where the simple relationships given in Table 2.4 exist.

19   At distances close to a source of electromagnetic fields, ie where the source does not effectively act as a point at the observation position, the angular distribution of the energy radiated varies with distance and this region is called the radiating near field where a complex field distribution exists. Constructive and destructive interference effects can arise where the antenna is large compared to the wavelength. At closer distances and well within a wavelength a region called the reactive near field exists where non-radiating field components may be dominant. In both cases, ie the radiating and reactive near fields, the electric and magnetic fields need to be assessed independently.

20   With respect to human exposure, the practical significance of the near field is where the wavelength is long with respect to the dimensions of the human body or where there is relatively close approach to a source. This applies primarily in the ELF to VHF range. At the lower frequencies, particularly those used for power distribution, the wavelength is several thousand kilometres and the exposure of people is assessed by separate measurement of the electric and magnetic fields.

21   At sufficient distances and at higher frequencies, where power density is a useful concept, measurement of the electric field strength alone would permit determination of magnetic field strength. At frequencies such as those used for microwave transmissions, where wavelengths are short with respect to the dimensions of the antenna and people, it is reasonable to think in terms of radiated fields.

22   Examples of fields to which people are exposed are given in Table 2.5.

EXPOSURE ASSESSMENT

Dosimetry

23   Whilst the objective of this chapter is to provide an overview of the exposure to electric and magnetic fields external to the body, it is important to realise that many of the effects of exposure can be related to the response to electric fields and currents induced in tissues. Dosimetric concepts have been developed which

Exposure condition	Electric field strength	Magnetic flux density
Environmental — natural fields		
Static, fair weather	120-150 V m^{-1}	50 µT
Static, stormy weather	10 kV m^{-1}	50 µT
Environmental — human activities		
50 Hz, 400 kV power line, midspan	10 kV m^{-1}	40 µT
50 Hz, 400 kV power line, 25 m from midspan	1 kV m^{-1}	8 µT
500-1600 kHz, 100 m from AM broadcast antenna	20 V m^{-1}	—
27 MHz, 4 W CB radio, 12 cm from antenna	100-600 V m^{-1}	0.25-1.0 µT
470-854 MHz, TV broadcast, maximum within 1 km of TV mast	3 V m^{-1}	0.1 µT
Home/work related		
Static, 30 cm from TV/VDU	0.5-10 kV m^{-1}	—
50 Hz, ambient, distant appliances	1-10 V m^{-1}	0.01-1 µT
50 Hz, 30 cm from appliances	10-250 V m^{-1}	0.01-30 µT
3 cm from appliances	—	0.3-2000 µT
50 Hz, 0.5-1 m from induction furnaces	—	100-10 000 µT
50 Hz, substations etc	10-20 kV m^{-1}	Few hundred µT
15 kHz, 30 cm from TV/VDU	1-10 V m^{-1}	Up to 0.2 µT
0.15-10 kHz, 0.1-1 m from induction heaters	—	15-1250 µT
250-675 kHz, at operator positions from induction heaters	2-100 V m^{-1}	0.2-22 µT
10-80 MHz, 15 cm from dielectric heaters	20-800 V m^{-1}	0.1-1.1 µT
27-450 MHz, 5 cm from low power mobile antennas	200-1350 V m^{-1}	—
470-854 MHz, TV aerial riggers	30-300 V m^{-1}	0.1-1.3 µT
		Power flux density
2450 MHz, 50 cm from microwave oven leaking at emission limit	14 V m^{-1}	0.5 W m^{-2}
2.82 GHz stationary ATC radar, off axis at 100 m	8 V m^{-1}	0.16 W m^{-2}
14 GHz satellite station off axis at 100 m	0.4 V m^{-1}	0.0004 W m^{-2}

TABLE 2.5
Examples of sources and field strengths to which people are exposed

provide a basis for linking external electric and magnetic fields to the electric field strength, induced current density and the energy absorption rate in tissues[3–6].

24   At the ELF frequencies used for power distribution, internal electric field strengths are about one-million times smaller than the external field strength. For every kilovolt per metre of external field strength a current is induced in the body which is proportional to the surface area of the body and for an average adult is about $14\,\mu A$. Current densities which depend on the conductivity of the body tissues range from 80 to $250\,\mu A\,m^{-2}$ in the head and trunk. Figure 2.2a illustrates the induced current flowing to ground when a person is exposed to a vertical electric field. Magnetic fields induce circulating current loops in the body, the current density depending on the radius of the loop and the conductivity of the tissues. At a frequency of $50\,Hz$ a $1\,\mu T$ horizontal magnetic field will induce a current density of about $5\,\mu A\,m^{-2}$ in the surface tissues of a standing adult person. The mechanism of magnetic field coupling is shown in Figure 2.2b.

25   Whilst current density is the quantity most clearly related to the biological effects at low frequencies, it is the energy absorption rate which becomes the

FIGURE 2.2
Induced currents in the body from exposure to ELF electric and magnetic fields

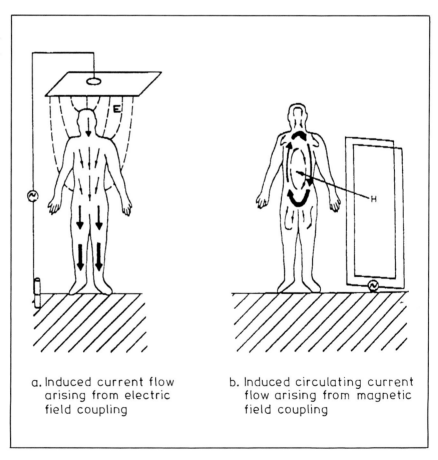

a. Induced current flow arising from electric field coupling

b. Induced circulating current flow arising from magnetic field coupling

more significant quantity as frequencies increase, towards wavelengths which become comparable to the human body dimensions. The energy absorption rate is proportional to the square of the internal electric field strength or current density and, if sufficient energy is absorbed, measurable temperature rises will occur. The term used to describe energy absorption rate is the specific absorption rate (SAR) for which the unit is watt per kilogram (W kg^{-1}).

26   SAR may be specified as the value normalised over the whole body mass (sometimes referred to as the 'whole body averaged SAR') or the localised value over a small mass of tissue ('localised SAR'). The localised SAR is important from two standpoints: the resulting non-uniform distribution of energy absorption when exposed to a uniform plane wave, and the localised energy absorption arising from non-uniform fields in close proximity to a source of exposure. For a given irradiation condition, the relationship between the whole body averaged value and localised distribution of SAR will be maintained.

27   As the frequencies reach the HF/VHF band, the orientation of the body with respect to the incident field becomes increasingly important, the body behaving as an antenna and absorbing energy in a resonant manner which depends on the length of the body with respect to the wavelength. For an adult who is electrically isolated from ground, the peak of this resonant absorption occurs in the frequency range 70–80 MHz and about half this value for someone who is electrically grounded. Smaller people and children show the resonance characteristic at higher frequencies. An example of calculations of SAR for electrically grounded adults and children is given in Figure 2.3 after Dimbylow[7]. Resonant effects also arise at higher frequencies for parts of the body such as the head.

28   As the frequency increases above the resonance region, power absorption becomes increasingly confined to the surface layers of the body and is essentially confined to the skin above a few tens of gigahertz.

29   The internal quantities, such as electric field strength, current density or temperature rise, are of primary importance when considering the effects of exposure; however, these are not easily measurable quantities as they often require the use of invasive probes. The use of such probes is not a generally accepted method of ascertaining the extent of human exposure and consequently such devices and techniques are usually relegated to models of humans (phantoms).

30   It is for these reasons that exposure assessments are generally carried out with reference to external field quantities and that whilst protection guidelines are founded on fundamental restrictions on current, current density and SAR[8–11], they are supported by a framework of external field strength values which provide varying degrees of conservatism. The assessments may be achieved by calculation, the use of some form of surrogate for exposure, reference to similar exposure, or measurement. Calculation usually involves simplifying assumptions which may not accurately reflect the reality of exposure and there may be considerable uncertainty attached to the use of surrogates for exposure, such as hours on duty or distance of residence from a wiring configuration.

31   The only definitive way of ascertaining exposure in many situations is to carry out measurements using appropriate instrumentation. In some circumstances it is

FIGURE 2.3
*Specific absorption
rates (SARs) for
electrically
grounded adults
and children in the
whole body
resonance region*

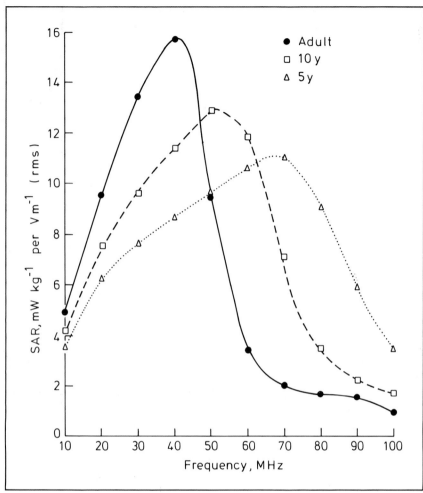

possible to measure directly the magnitude of induced currents within the body[12]. Generally, however, the only practicable approach is to measure the external electric or magnetic field strengths. Even so there are many difficulties to address in assessing exposure from an external field strength or body current measurement, not the least of which is the time for which people are exposed at the positions where measurements are made and the effect of non-uniform or partial body exposure. These difficulties are reflected in the uncertainty of exposure assessment.

Instrumentation and methods

ELF field measurements

32 Electric field strength measurements are most commonly made by measuring the induced current flowing between two electrically insulated halves of a metallic shell which is generally spherical or rectangular in shape[13]. Amplifiers mounted within the probe body provide a self-contained instrument with either inbuilt metering or remote metering using fibre-optic coupled readout stations to minimise field perturbation. It is normally the root mean square (RMS) value of the electric field strength which is recorded when the separated halves of the probe are aligned with the electric field component. Calibration of such instruments can be achieved using parallel plate systems to set up a uniform field to an accuracy of about 1%. However, in practice it is unlikely that measurement uncertainty will be better than 10% given the perturbation arising from people and objects in the field. A person close to the instrument can seriously affect the local field distribution and, as a consequence, the instrument reading, the magnitude of the effect depending on the local field conditions. The effect of the proximity of the person carrying out measurements is likely to be less than 5% for distances greater than 1.5 m from the instrument.

33   Magnetic field strength measurements are made using coils which are designed to shield against the effect of any electric field component. The rate of change of magnetic flux through the area intercepted by the coil results in an induced electromotive force from which the magnetic flux density can be ascertained by using an appropriate voltmeter. Instruments have been designed with orthogonal loops to provide independence of field orientation and, unlike electric field strength measurements, field perturbation causes minimal problems for measurements in practice. Accurate calibration of magnetic field strength instruments can be achieved by using Helmholtz coils which can be designed to provide a uniform magnetic field over the volume occupied by the measuring instrument.

34   A recent development which is of considerable interest for epidemiological studies is that of the personal dosemeter which has been designed to log continuously the electric and magnetic field exposure of the wearer. The simplest type of instrument is a magnetic field dosemeter which weighs only about 110 g and relies upon an electrolytic cell to store the accumulated charge from a three-axis magnetic field sensor instrument. The time integral of the magnetic field exposure (μT h) is obtained by measuring the total charge. This type of instrument is useful for evaluating time weighted average exposure but does not provide information on the variation of magnetic flux density with time and is therefore of limited value in any investigation of postulated threshold effects of exposure. At the forefront of ELF personal dosemeter technology are instruments weighing 200–300 g which can measure orthogonal magnetic field components including harmonics to 800 Hz and the electric field strength at the surface of the body. Sampling intervals range upwards from about one second and the information can be logged continuously over several days depending on the sampling rate. When downloaded on to a personal computer the data can be analysed using comprehensive statistical software packages. An example of the output from one such instrument (EMDEX II) is shown in Figure 2.4.

RF field measurements

35   Instruments used to measure RF field strengths for comparison with the reference levels, or limits given in protection guidelines, usually have broadband characteristics, ie possess a relatively frequency independent response over a

FIGURE 2.4 *Magnetic flux density recorded by 50 Hz personal dosemeter*

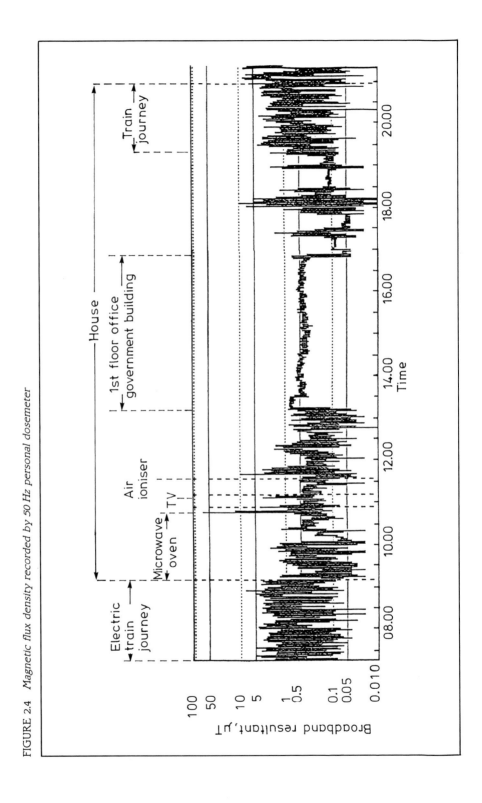

16

defined bandwidth. Where high sensitivity is required, such as in the quantification of field strengths at levels below protection guidelines limits, narrow-band systems are used and signals from calibrated antennas are fed into spectrum analysers or field strength meters.

36   The prescription by Bowman[14,15], of the desirable characteristics required of broadband instrumentation for the surveying of hazards, has formed the basis of many commercial developments[16,17]. Instruments are available which: measure E or H fields; have sensors which are much smaller than the shortest wavelength to be measured; cause minimal scattering of the field; are independent of orientation using orthogonal loop or dipole antennas; have wide dynamic ranges; have automatic zeroing capability in the field. The additional development of data logging facilities has further improved the capabilities of such instruments.

37   Notwithstanding improvements in instrument design, it is unlikely that the accuracy of the measurements will be better than ± 30%.

38   With simple far-field exposure, power density (S) may be a meaningful quantity but in complicated fields, such as interference and reactive near fields, it is easier to measure the magnitudes of E and H. The far-field relationships in Table 2.4 are used to determine the power density from instruments which generally incorporate sensors detecting either the electric or magnetic field strength. The sensors for electric fields tend to be dipoles and for magnetic fields, loops or coils. Any single dipole or loop will be polarisation sensitive, responding to the appropriate component of the field. An isotropic response (equal in all directions) is approached by the use of three sensors mounted at right angles, although in practice there is likely to be a small degree of anisotropy.

39   In complex near-field zones where the free space impedance of 377 Ω may not be a valid assumption, the electric (or magnetic) field strength can be obtained from an indicated power density reading from the above relationships. Instruments have been manufactured to display in terms of field strength or (field strength)^2 corresponding to sensor capability and relevant to advised reference levels or limits. An instrument has also been designed to match the frequency response of the protection guidelines[18]. In addition to the range of instruments used for external field measurements[19], very small electric field probes have also been developed for dosimetric purposes[20,21].

FIELD EXPOSURES
General considerations

40   When considering the exposure to electric and magnetic fields arising from various sources it is important to appreciate that exposure to fields generated at one frequency is not directly comparable to exposure at other frequencies. This may be particularly relevant when considering occupational exposure where electric and magnetic fields from a variety of sources may be encountered.

41   Electric and magnetic field measurements relevant to the assessment of personal exposure are either environmental or personal. The majority of assessments made to date involve environmental measurements at specific

locations. The use of the spatial and temporal characteristics of specific sources, eg rotating radar systems or non-uniform field distributions close to some sources, provides a means to ascertain exposure, although detailed knowledge of occupancy is not always available. Data logging facilities coupled to instruments suitable for environmental measurements have improved the exposure assessment capability in some specific situations where there is marked spatial variation in field strength and where occupancy is intermittent[22].

42   It is still far from clear as to what measure would be most appropriate for estimating the risk of some of the possible effects on humans that have been postulated. The most appropriate measure at ELF frequencies is commonly assumed to be time weighted average exposure, but there is no firm evidence that this is, in fact, so. It is therefore not surprising that personal dosimetry has not developed in a manner similar to that of ionising radiation. In addition, there are significant problems in interpreting measurements where wavelengths can range from being very much greater to very much less than the body dimensions and where the response of antennas close to the body may be very different from that in free space. Nonetheless, as mentioned in paragraph 34, techniques for personal dosimetry at ELF frequencies are being developed and may extend to other parts of the spectrum.

Power frequency fields

43   People are exposed to fields from the transmission, distribution and use of electricity at 50 Hz in Western Europe and 60 Hz in North America. The ubiquitous nature of power frequency electric and magnetic fields is one of the reasons why it is difficult to make distinctions between exposures at work and at home. Various groups may be the focus of particular interest because of their proximity to specific sources of exposure, such as local power lines and substations, or because of their use of electrical appliances; but these sources are not necessarily the dominant contributors to their time weighted average exposure[23].

Electric fields

44   *Sources of exposure*   High voltage power lines give rise to the highest electric field strengths that are likely to be encountered by people. The value of maximum electric field strength[24] immediately under the highest voltage transmission line of 400 kV in the UK is about 11 kV m^{-1} at the minimum clearance of 7.6 m, although, in general, people will be exposed to fields well below this level. At 25 m lateral displacement from the midspan position the field strength is about 1 kV m^{-1}. Table 2.6 illustrates the field strength directly beneath and at 25 m lateral displacement for 400, 275 and 132 kV lines.

45   Objects such as trees and other electrically grounded objects will introduce screening effects and will substantially reduce the electric field strength in their vicinity. Inside buildings electric field strengths from transmission lines will be reduced by factors of between 10 and 100. Electric field exposure will then be due to fields arising from proximity to wiring and appliances.

46   *Exposure: workers*   Some workers in the power transmission and distribution industry may be exposed to electric field strengths above 11 kV m^{-1} but in the

Location	Electric field strength (kV m^{-1}) near power line of:			TABLE 2.6
	400 kV	275 kV	132 kV	*Electric field strengths near power lines*
Maximum at ground level for minimum conductor clearance	11	6	2	
25 m lateral displacement from centreline	1	0.2	0.05	

occupational environment it is possible to control exposure by the introduction of screening.

47   The use of personal dosemeters to evaluate the exposure of people at work in Canada was reported by Deadman *et al*[25]. Occupational and residential exposures of electricity supply utility workers and a comparison group of office workers were monitored over approximately a 1 week period. The utility workers were classified into six occupational groups and the time averaged electric field strength as determined at the body surface was found to be considerably higher for distribution linemen, apparatus technicians and transmission linemen. The mean exposure for each of these three groups at work was 62.5, 181.7, and 418.9 V m^{-1}, respectively, as against a background group field strength of 4.9 V m^{-1}. To illustrate the variability of exposure, the electricians involved with repair and maintenance of substations had daily exposures which ranged from 7.4 to 1756.3 V m^{-1}. At work, the mean electric field strength for all exposed groups was 48.3 V m^{-1}, the factor of 10 difference between work exposure and background exposure being reduced to 1.7 when the effect of combining home and work exposure over a period of 1 week was taken into account.

48   *Exposure: public*   Electric field strength exposure exceeds 1 kV m^{-1} only close to high voltage lines. In the home and in buildings where the supply voltage is reduced to 240 V (UK), electric field strengths in the centre of rooms are generally in the range 1−10 V m^{-1}, and close to domestic appliances and cables this may increase to 200−300 V m^{-1}.

Magnetic fields

49   *Sources of exposure*   Unlike electric fields where the highest exposures are likely to be experienced close to high voltage transmission lines, the highest magnetic flux densities are more likely to be in the vicinity of equipment that is carrying large currents.

50   The maximum magnetic flux densities encountered close to UK overhead cables are summarised in Table 2.7. For comparison, Tables 2.8 and 2.9 illustrate the range of magnetic flux densities encountered in both occupational and domestic settings. Occupational exposure to induction heating and arc welding, where high currents are used, are treated more extensively in paragraphs 60−72.

51   *Exposure: workers*   A survey of exposure to power frequency magnetic fields experienced by electricity supply industry staff in the UK[28] illustrated that most exposure (time weighted average) arose at work, irrespective of whether the

TABLE 2.7
Magnetic flux densities near power lines

Location	Magnetic flux density (µT) near power line of:		
	400 kV	275 kV	132 kV
Maximum at ground level directly beneath power line	40	22	10
25 m lateral displacement from centreline	8	4	2

TABLE 2.8
Occupational exposures to power frequency magnetic fields

Occupation	Range of magnetic flux densities (µT)	Reference
Electronics assemblers, microelectronics	0.001-0.006	26
Radio operators	0.02-0.04	26
Electronics assemblers, soldering	0.13-0.16	26
VDU operators	0.10-0.72	27,53
Power industry, managerial*	0.22-1.18	28
Power industry, administrative/clerical*	0.08-1.40	28
Radio and TV repairers	0.1-2.6	26
Electronics assemblers, sputtering	1.4-4.3	26
Power industry, industrial*	0.07-4.60	28
Power industry, distribution (<75 kV) linesmen*	0.41-5.40	25
Power industry, splicers, distribution lines (<25 kV)*	0.68-6.36	25
Power industry, apparatus electricians/mechanics*	0.53-6.45	25
Power industry, scientific/engineering*	0.18-8.34	28
Power industry, transmission(>300 kV) linesmen*	1.21-24.8	25, 29
Arc welders	$0.5-10^3$	30
Induction furnace workers	Up to 10^4	31

*Data were obtained using personal dosemeters.

TABLE 2.9
Typical domestic exposures to magnetic fields

Conditions	Magnetic flux density range (µT)	Reference
Average personal domestic exposure*	0.026-0.493	28
Ambient domestic fields†	0.040-1.3	28, 32
Ambient domestic fields, electric heating	0.6-12	32, 33
During use of an electric blanket	1.6-3.6	34, 35

* Measured using a personal dosemeter. The mean value of 0.135 µT was more than a factor of two higher than the mean established on the basis of static (environmental) measurements.
† Other studies have also indicated values within this range.

groups were amongst the highest exposed on operational sites, ie generation and transmission, or the lowest exposed on other sites, ie showroom or headquarters staff. Table 2.10 (after Renew *et al*[8]) is based on information presented at the 1990 meeting of Cigré and provides a breakdown of the contribution to exposure from various activities taking account of the time for which the activity arose. The implication for people who work in the electricity supply industry is that approximately 70% of total exposure arises at work, 20% at home and about 10% travelling and at other places.

52 For 75 people working on operational sites the mean exposure was about 955 nT but the individual exposures ranged from 65 to 8381 nT during the course of the monitoring period which lasted for a week. Measurements made in homes ranged from 2.5 to 171 nT and up to about 500 nT when high voltage transmission lines were within 100 m of the home.

53 The exposure of people in the generation, transmission and distribution of electricity and particularly of those involved in repair and maintenance work is of special interest. From the study using personal dosemeters by Deadman *et al*[5] the mean magnetic flux densities at work for the six occupational groups ranged from 1140 to 3440 nT, whereas the range of exposure for apparatus electricians varied from 770 to 18 480 nT. The mean of all occupational groups was 1660 nT compared with the background group of 160 nT. This factor of 10 difference was reduced to 3.5 when the dilution effect of home exposures of the occupationally exposed groups (over a period of 1 week) was taken into account.

Job	Activity (%)					Average exposure (nT) over 1 week (Range for individuals)	Number
	At home in bed	At home up	Out	Travel to work	At work		
Scientific and engineering	6	12	7	7	68	274 (80-795)	13
Administrative and clerical	8	14	6	3	69	156 (49-399)	11
Industrial	9	14	5	2	70	304 (55-659)	16
Managerial	4	9	9	2	76	203 (125-281)	2
All	7	13	6	4	70	256 (49-795)	42

TABLE 2.10
Partial exposure for different activities over a range of job categories expressed as percentage of weekly mean

54   *Exposure: public* Kavet *et al*[36] carried out a comparative study in Maine using both spot and personal dosemeters to assess the exposure of 45 men who lived close to (within 300 feet — about 90 m) and those who lived remote from (further than 700 feet — about 215 m) overhead power lines. In practice, measurements confirmed that of the 30 men said to be living close to the lines, 5 lived further away, the furthest distance being 465 feet (140 m). Men selected for the study were those who lived close to existing 345 kV *plus* 115 kV lines within the same right of way, those who lived close to 115 kV lines alone, and those who lived remotely. The groups were in some cases subdivided according to the number of 115 kV lines within the right of way and on which side of the right of way they lived, ie closer to the 345 or 115 kV lines. On the basis of spot measurements at the selected residences subgroups were aggregated into four classification groups to establish a gradient of exposure due to fields from the overhead power lines.

55   Personal dosemeters were then used for a 24 h weekday period in the summer to investigate the effect of exposures away from home on total exposure. Table 2.11 (after Kavet *et al*) is a summary of the personal exposure measurements for the four groups, excluding the record of one participant because of the skew effect on the data of a high workplace exposure. The mean exposure of the others away from home was about 200 nT but the range was 80—360 nT.

56   One of the conclusions of the study is that caution should be used in characterising exposure on the basis of environmental measurements. Neither home exposures nor total time weighted average exposures from personal dosemeter measurements corresponded in close hierarchical order with the spot

TABLE 2.11
Summary of personal exposure assessment for four exposure groups remote from and close to 345 kV and 115 kV transmission lines

	Magnetic flux density (nT)					
	At home		Away from home		Total (time weighted average)	
Group*	Mean	Standard deviation	Mean	Standard deviation	Mean	Standard deviation
Remote	159	104	198	79	157	69
I	112	32	177	70	126	29
II	242	165	221	68	241	119
III†	318	112	180	20	259	54

*Group description

Remote — More than 700 feet (215 m) from any transmission line.

I   — Within 300 feet (90 m) of 115 kV line and on 115 kV side of right of way (ROW) with both 345 kV line and a single 115 kV line.

II   — On 115 kV line side of a ROW containing a 345 kV line and 2 × 115 kV lines and on 345 kV line side of a ROW containing a 345 kV line and a single 115 kV line.

III   — On 345 kV line side of a ROW containing a 345 kV line and 2 × 115 kV lines.

†Excludes one abnormal exposure away from home.

TABLE 2.12
Power frequency magnetic flux densities at various distances from examples of household appliances

Appliance	Magnetic flux density (µT) at a distance of:		
	3 cm	30 cm	1 m
Can openers	1000-2000	3.5-30	0.07-1
Clothes dryers	0.3-8	0.08-0.3	0.02-0.06
Clothes washers	0.8-50	0.15-3	0.01-0.15
Dishwashers	3.5-20	0.6-3	0.07-0.3
Drills	400-800	2-3.5	0.08-0.2
Fluorescent desk lamps	40-400	0.5-2	0.02-0.25
Food mixers	60-700	0.6-10	0.02-0.25
Hair dryers	6-2000	<0.01-7	<0.01-0.3
Irons	8-30	0.12-0.3	0.01-0.025
Microwave ovens	75-200	4-8	0.25-0.6
Ovens (conventional)	1-50	0.15-0.5	0.01-0.04
Portable heaters	10-180	0.15-5	0.01-0.25
Refrigerators	0.5-1.7	0.01-0.25	<0.01
Shavers	15-1500	0.08-9	<0.01-0.3
Television sets	2.5-50	0.04-2	<0.01-0.15
Toasters	7-18	0.06-0.7	<0.01
Vacuum cleaners	200-800	2-20	0.13-2

measurements; the latter overestimated the inter-group exposure ratio as determined by the personal dosemeters. Whilst there was some overlap in the range of exposures received by highest exposed category (group III) and those who lived remotely, the difference between the mean exposures of the groups was significant.

57   In a study of 41 homes Belanger *et al*[37] reported a mean exposure in houses of 120 nT when instrumentation was placed away from appliances, the variation between rooms being in the range 7–150 nT.

58   The highest magnetic flux densities to which most people are exposed arise close to domestic appliances which incorporate motors, transformers and heaters. The flux density changes rapidly with distance from appliances and, whereas at 1 m distance the flux density will be of the same order as the background levels, eg 10–300 nT, at 3 cm distance magnetic flux densities may be as high as 2 mT from devices such as hair dryers and can openers[38]. The results of the study are shown in Table 2.12 which indicates that there can be wide variations in flux densities from similar appliances.

59   Whereas exposure to most household appliances is intermittent, exposure to magnetic fields from electric over-blankets can be prolonged. The flux density for a 1 cm blanket/body separation is in the range 2000–3000 nT and in the range 50–450 nT for the head[35].

Induction heating (50 Hz — 1 MHz)

Sources of exposure

60   The highest workplace magnetic field strengths from power frequencies, and harmonics, arise in industries which utilise equipment having a high current demand, notably close to arc-welding equipment and induction furnaces.

61   Induced alternating currents to heat conducting materials, such as metals and crystals, are used extensively in industry for a variety of purposes, such as drying, bonding, surface hardening, zone refining, annealing, brazing and melting. The frequency and power used depend on the process requirements but the important parameter in choice of frequency is the skin depth or depth of penetration of the field. Frequencies used vary from 50 Hz to about 1 MHz and powers range from about 1 kW to several MW for induction furnaces. The higher frequencies tend to be used for surface treatments where the skin depth is low, whereas the lower frequencies are used for volume heating and for melting. The coils may be small, single-turn devices of a few cm diameter used for heating localised regions of a product to large, multiturn systems of 1 or 2 m diameter such as those used in induction furnaces capable of melting several tons of iron.

Exposure

62   Measurements made on induction furnaces and heaters operating in the frequency range from 50 Hz to 10 kHz are summarised[31] in Table 2.13. The measured fields reflect the variation in time and space of fields to which the operators might be exposed; they are not an assessment of operator exposure. The high field strengths recorded for the induction heaters arise from the measurements made very close (10 cm) to the applicator coils.

63   From another study[39] of induction heaters in the frequency range from 180 Hz to 10 kHz, magnetic flux densities close to 25 machines ranged from 15 to 1300 μT at positions close to the equipment which may be compared to hand exposure of 590 μT to 25 mT arising from the use of portable equipment operating over a similar frequency band.

64   At higher frequencies of 300–500 kHz, operator exposure to 16 induction heaters[40], of nominal RF output powers ranging from 2.5 to 50 kW, indicated that the magnetic flux densities were in the range <0.1–22 μT.

TABLE 2.13
Magnetic flux densities associated with induction furnaces

Machine	Number of machines	Measurement distance (m)	Frequency band (Hz)	Magnetic flux density measured range (μT)
Ladle furnace in conjunction with 1.6 Hz magnetic stirrer	1	0.5-1.0	1.6, 50	200-10 000
Induction furnace	2	0.6-0.9	50	100-900
	5	0.8-2.0	600	100-900
Channel furnace	3	0.6-3.0	50	100-400
Induction heater	5	0.1-1.0	50-10 000	1 000-60 000

65   The electric field strengths would appear to be of little practical significance where induction heaters are concerned and, in general, are no more than a few tens of volts per metre at accessible positions.

66   There is very little information on working practices which determines the time spent at the positions where measurements are made. When manual operations are carried out, this is clearly an important element in determining exposure given the rapid variation in field strength at distances less than 50 cm from small coils.

Arc welding and cutting (50/60 Hz and harmonics)

Sources of exposure

67   Arc welding and cutting is performed using a variety of methods, which require the use of large currents. Both direct current (DC) and alternating current (AC) equipment is used and in some cases high frequencies are superimposed to strike or maintain the arc. The type of arc welder of particular interest is the 50/60 Hz power frequency AC welder. Gas–tungsten arc welding (GTAW) or tungsten–inert-gas (TIG) arc welding may use currents of less than 50 A when welding soft metals, whereas high power plasma arc-cutting devices may use up to 1000 A. With arc welding, the arc, cables, and welding equipment are close to the welder and cables can touch the body.

Exposure

68   Stuchly and Lecuyer[30] reported measurements of electric and magnetic fields close to arc-welding equipment and whilst the maximum field strength was generally at the fundamental frequency, in some cases a harmonic was dominant.

69   Table 2.14 gives a summary of the range of RMS magnetic flux densities at various anatomical positions, the measurement coil placed at 10 cm from the body of the welder.

70   In addition to the observed range of maximum magnetic flux density of 200 µT to 1 mT at various parts of the anatomy, there will also be a gradient of magnetic flux density with distance from the source at a given body position. The rapid change in magnetic flux density with distance from the cables is an important aspect of evaluating exposure where cables may be in contact with the body.

71   Electric field strengths where measurable were generally a few tens of volts per metre.

	Magnetic flux density (µT)		
Part of body	Mean	Minimum	Maximum
Head	66	0.4	200
Chest	90	3.8	263
Waist	175	0.5	438
Gonads	173	2.5	625
Hand	166	3.8	1000
Leg	144	5.0	375

TABLE 2.14
Range of magnetic flux densities at 10 cm from different parts of the body of arc welders

72   The difficulties of assessing exposure to this type of equipment are primarily associated with the non-uniform fields, evaluating harmonic content and taking account of working practices.

Dielectric heating (10—100 MHz)

Sources of exposure

73   Machines used for RF dielectric heating are one of the most significant sources of RF exposure amongst the working population and have been the focus of some attention[41-43]. The wavelength range in air of this type of equipment is 3—30 m, thus exposure occurs well within a wavelength of the source where complex field distributions occur. Dielectric heaters have output powers ranging from less than 1 kW to tens of kW and can be completely shielded and automated or be unshielded and operated manually. In general, the greatest exposure arises from machines of a few kW used for welding PVC where, in particular, operators of machines using C-frame presses to weld PVC often sit 30—50 cm from the welding electrodes.

Exposure

74   Electric field strengths can be up to 500 V m^{-1} at the positions of the trunk, and hands may be placed in regions where the field strength exceeds 1 kV m^{-1}. Magnetic flux densities vary from less than 100 nT to about 500 nT at the position of the trunk, whereas the hands may be transiently exposed to fields of several μT.

75   The RF grounding of the frame of the machines can significantly affect the current distribution on the machine and therefore the magnetic field generated. In addition, the spatial distribution of electric field strength at positions occupied by the operators is highly non-uniform, resulting in reduced energy absorption rate in the near field[44].

76   The problems of evaluating exposure to this type of equipment are complicated by the nature of the work. The weld cycle is usually a matter of seconds and the duty factor (RF on time to total cycle time) can vary from about 0.1 to 0.5. During each weld cycle the field strengths vary and the operators may need to place their hands in regions of high field strength.

77   At the frequencies used for RF dielectric heating it is possible to obtain a measure of the currents induced in the body resulting from exposure to the electric fields[45]. The development of approaches using induced current provides an improved indicator of exposure. This is particularly so when the current measurements are coupled to the current distribution in the body using mathematical models, an approach which is presently being developed[7,46].

Antenna fields (3 kHz — 3 GHz)

Fixed and mobile sources

78   Antennas generate electromagnetic fields across the spectrum. At very low frequencies (VLF), the structures are massive with support towers of 200—250 m high and the fields may be extensive over the site area. Electric field strengths of several hundred volts per metre may be encountered within the boundary defined by the antenna structures. Magnetic flux densities in the range 3—18 μT have been measured close to VLF antenna feeds and 0.3—65 μT close to LF towers. In transmitter buildings magnetic flux densities were in the range from 0.1 nT to 14 μT.

79   Measurements and calculations through these frequency bands and up to about 100 MHz have been made of induced currents related to external field strengths under uniform field exposure conditions. The short-circuit currents rise to a theoretical maximum of 10—12 mA per V m^{-1} at the resonance frequency of around 35 MHz for an ideally electrically grounded adult[7,47] and measurements indicate that, under normal exposure conditions, the current is reduced to about 6—8 mA per V m^{-1}.

80   At close distances to attennas with respect to their physical dimensions, field distributions can be non-uniform. This is particularly so for mobile and portable systems where the field strengths change rapidly with distance from the antenna. Electric field strengths of about 1300 V m^{-1} have been measured at 5 cm from 4 W citizens' band transmitters[48], whereas at 60 cm the field strengths fall to less than 60 V m^{-1}.

81   In the USA, a study of population exposure to background fields from VHF and UHF broadcast transmitters[49] showed that the median exposure for 15 cities was 50 μW m^{-2}, although some cities had median exposures of 200 μW m^{-2} and maximum exposures, which were from local FM radio stations, were about 0.1 W m^{-2}.

Hand-held transceivers

82   The use of hand-held communications systems is growing rapidly and, whilst the powers of new generation devices aimed to reach millions of people are likely to be less than 1 W, the powers of some existing transmitters may be several watts. Existing cellphone frequencies are around 900 MHz but a proposed Digital European Cordless Telephony (DECT) system will use frequencies around 1.8 GHz. At about 1 cm from a 1 W, VHF antenna, field strengths of 1700 V m^{-1} may be deduced[50]; however, it is clear that external electric field strengths in the absence of a body cannot be used as a ready measure of exposure in circumstances where the antenna is used in close proximity to the head. The approach taken to determine exposure in humans has been to use models and assess the internal dosimetric quantity as a function of the power fed to the antenna[50-52].

83   Exposure assessment is clearly not a simple matter under these circumstances and is further complicated by the transmit duty factor.

Visual display units (VDUs) (50—70 Hz, 15—30 kHz and harmonics)

84   VDUs as computer displays are found in virtually every workplace and in many homes. Whilst interest has focused on the emissions from VDUs in view of the proximity of people to the equipment, television sets generate similar fields. Electric and magnetic fields are produced in the ELF and VLF bands from the power supply and the linescan and screen refresh generators. The horizontal linescan frequency is in the VLF band, usually between 15 and 30 kHz, although harmonics up to several hundred kHz can be produced. Measurements made at operator positions about 30—50 cm from the screen indicate that the ELF and VLF electric field strengths are in the range 1—10 V m^{-1}, although close to the surfaces of the equipment field strengths may be 200–300 V m^{-1}. The VLF magnetic flux density at operator distances is in the range 20–140 nT, whereas ELF magnetic flux densities tend to be higher[53–55], in the region of 100–700 nT. Close to the casing of VDUs, VLF magnetic flux densities can be several μT.

Microwave ovens (2.45 GHz)

85   Microwave ovens are manufactured to standards which require that leakage levels are kept below emission limits. In the UK, British Standard 3456: 1988[56] requires that microwave leakage should not exceed 50 W m^{-2} at 5 cm from the external surface of the appliance. If the leakage arises from an isolated point such as a small slot in the oven door periphery, the exposure at distances occupied by people will be very much lower than the emission level measured at 5 cm. In addition, the fields will be non-uniform over the body at close distances of approach. It is for these reasons that it is important that product emission standards should not be confused with exposure standards or guidelines.

86   In a recent UK survey[57] of 357 microwave ovens used in the catering industry, of which 208 were of the domestic type, 6 ovens indicated leakage above 10 W m^{-2} and 1 oven did not meet the 50 W m^{-2} emission standard. Leakage of 10 W m^{-2} at 5 cm from a single point implies an exposure of 0.1 W m^{-2} at 50 cm and 0.25 mW m^{-2} at 1 m.

Terrestrial and satellite microwave links, radar (0.5–200 GHz)

87   Point-to-point microwave communications links and many of the satellite communications antennas are in fixed positions but the principles of exposure assessment would apply to mobile systems. Similar considerations apply to radars, which operate at microwave frequencies but transmit short pulses of 1 μs or less. Peak powers in the pulses may be more than one-thousand times greater than the average power.

88   Terrestrial and satellite link antennas generally use parabolic reflectors of circular cross-section. The diameters can vary from less than 1 m up to 60 m, with many falling in the range 5–15 m. The large reflector diameter to wavelength ratios for these dishes and radar reflectors result in gains ranging from 30 to 80 dB depending on the particular system. Power output for line of sight links may be less than 1 W to a few W, whereas powers may vary from a few hundred watt to more than 1 kW for satellite links or high power radar. The narrow beamwidth of rotating radars such as those used for air traffic control give rise to intermittent exposure. Various approaches have been used to estimate the potential exposure to fields from such antennas[58,59] and to determine the near-field and far-field boundaries. Dependent on the system it is possible to be exposed to fields of a few hundred W m^{-2} in the near field of high power stations; but given that antennas are directed at satellites, at terrestrial receivers situated well above ground level or at aircraft, etc, and nearby buildings have to be avoided, exposure to the main lobe is unlikely to arise close to the transmitting antennas. Only people who have access to the vicinity of the reflector or approach the useful beam at low elevation angles are likely to be exposed to fields in the order of a few tens of W m^{-2}. Outside of the geometric projection of the reflector, the fields will be reduced by factors of

100 or greater, which means that, in most cases, public exposure at normally accessible positions will be typically below 10^{-3} W m^{-2} at distances in excess of 100 m measured along the antenna axis.

EXPOSURE ASSESSMENT AND EPIDEMIOLOGY

89   Paragraphs 40—88 outlined the magnitude of electromagnetic fields from the most common sources to which people are exposed. Some of the problems of exposure assessment have been identified, but the multiplicity of sources and modulations means that a complete characterisation of individual exposure in time and space is a complex matter.

90   For the purposes of comparing the exposures of the occupational groups defined by the Office of Population Censuses and Surveys (OPCS) in the UK, it is useful to divide them into three categories:

(1)   broad based groups for which information on the magnitude and type of exposure is not available and in many cases would be very difficult (if not impossible) to obtain — within these broad groupings there may be subgroups suitable for more detailed consideration;

(2)   specific occupations which would provide a good group for exposure assessment but for which there is little information at present;

(3)   specific occupations for which there is some information relevant to exposure assessment.

91   An example of a category (1) grouping would be electrical and electronic engineers, which covers a wide range of people who may be dealing solely with equipment operating at mains frequency and its harmonics to people dealing with equipment operating at frequencies throughout the RF spectrum. In many cases where RF sources are concerned there will also be the presence of power frequency fields. It will not be possible to ascertain the extent of exposure of people under such a broad category, although assessments could be carried out on identified subgroups. There is also the possibility that many engineers may be employed in design or production management capacities where exposure to electric and magnetic fields may not be materially different to non-electrical occupations.

92   Similarly, occupational groups classified as production fitters, electricians, TV and electronic maintenance fitters and mechanics could encompass a wide variation in the type of work carried out. It could range from those who do not work with 'live' equipment to those carrying out testing on operational systems. A problem with exposure assessment for people in the latter category is that the fields close to sources vary rapidly with distance from the equipment and give rise to partial body, non-uniform exposure.

93   There are specific subgroups, such as for those working on power generation and distribution, where some form of job classification could be used to identify different exposure bands to investigate the effect of exposure gradient. If job specification can be tied to exposure using the recently developed dosemeters, then it may be possible to carry out some form of retrospective study based on job specification. Power industry workers have been the subject of recent investigation and would therefore be more appropriately placed in category (2) or (3).

94   Other specific occupations which could fall in category (2) described above might be of people who use electrical appliances or who are exposed for long periods to electric and magnetic fields. Examples of such occupational groups are hairdressers, who make extensive use of hair dryers, and electric train drivers.

95   Category (3) occupational groups include arc welders, induction heater workers and operators of RF dielectric heating equipment. Measurements of field strengths to which these workers have been exposed were based on the recognition that they are amongst the most heavily occupationally exposed. Most measurements have been spot measurements. These can identify the maximum fields to which workers can be exposed but estimation of their time weighted average exposure requires knowledge of working practices and of the operating characteristics of the machines.

SUMMARY

Field measurements and exposure assessment

96   People are exposed to electromagnetic fields arising from numerous sources generating a wide range of frequencies and modulations. Not all sources of exposure have been identified in this review, but examples were selected to illustrate some of the problems of exposure assessment.

97   Spot measurements of field strength can be used to determine whether or not reference field strength levels are exceeded; however, the assessment of exposure requires further examination with respect to time and spatial averaging. This can be achieved by the use of instrumentation incorporating data logging facilities. Even so it may be difficult to relate field measurements to induced currents or specific absorption rate (SAR), as many exposures of practical significance arise in the near field of sources.

98   In the frequency range up to 100 MHz it is possible in some circumstances to obtain a measure of induced currents flowing in the body. Various approaches have been used to assess body currents and to relate external electric field strength with induced current as a function of frequency. In many practical situations, such as broadcast and other transmitter sites where people may be exposed to fields which give rise to measurable currents, the exposure situation is often complex and it is not a simple matter to determine internal current distribution from external current measurements.

99   The highest exposures arise close to sources where the fields are generally non-uniform and in these circumstances it is likely that only parts of the body are substantially exposed. This is one of the most problematical aspects of exposure assessment and, even with personal dosemeters, the full characterisation of exposure requires careful evaluation. This feature of non-uniform, partial body exposure arises both at home and at work close to

appliances and sources such as fixed and portable transmitting antennas, RF dielectric heaters, and arc-welding equipment.

100   Even in situations where exposure might be considered to be reasonably uniform over an extended period, such as the use of electric over-blankets, the degree of body coverage by the blanket will affect the average exposure.

101   The development of personal dosemeters such as those which are now available for ELF fields should result in a marked improvement in the assessment of exposure and similar developments are foreseeable for other frequencies.

Implications for epidemiology

102   This chapter has identified exposure to electric and magnetic fields emanating from a wide range of sources; however, it is clear that the primary concern of people has focused on the potential risks from power frequency magnetic fields.

103   The range of exposure to ELF magnetic fields in a number of occupations is summarised in Table 2.8 which indicates that the highest levels of exposure are likely to be encountered by arc welders and induction furnace workers. Groups working in the power generation and distribution industries may be worthy of further study as the improvements in personal dosimetry should provide the basis for establishing gradients of exposure.

104   People who live close to power transmission lines may be of particular interest but the effect of use and proximity to appliances and exposure away from home need also to be evaluated. Evidence suggests that even where gradients of magnetic flux density can be established for groups living in the vicinity of power lines, the time averaged exposure of people from the different groups may overlap and, where appropriate, exposure at work is likely to be the dominant contributor to exposure.

105   Appliances commonly regarded as domestic can be used extensively by various occupational groups, eg hairdressers who use hair dryers and industrial workers who use power tools. In these occupations electrical equipment is used regularly close to the body and yet the occupations are not regarded as electrical in character. For such groups, however, exposure could be reasonably well quantified and they might be suitable for epidemiological investigation.

106   Situations where prolonged rather than intermittent exposure to electromagnetic fields can arise include the use of electrical transport, electric over-blankets and underfloor electrical heating.

107   Arc welders are potentially amongst those workers with the highest occupational exposure to ELF magnetic fields. Exposure may, however, be difficult to assess because of its variation with distance from the welding arc and cables, and measurements need to be made with personal dosemeters. Exposure to other physical and chemical agents would also need to be taken into account in assessing any apparent occupational hazard.

108   Measurements close to induction furnaces show that those working with them are also potentially highly exposed. Again, however, measurements with personal dosemeters are required to obtain reasonably accurate estimates of exposure over time because of the natural restrictions on approach to the high temperature environment, coupled with the rapid fall off in magnetic flux density with distance from the source of exposure.

109 At higher frequencies, the operators of some types of dielectric heating equipment have been identified as perhaps the group most highly exposed to RF fields. The measurement of current induced in the body may lead to improved methods of exposure assessment.

REFERENCES

1   Repacholi, M H. Sources and applications of radiofrequency (RF) and microwave energy. IN *Biological Effects and Dosimetry of Non-ionizing Radiation, Radiofrequency and Microwave Energies* (M Grandolfo *et al*, eds). New York, Plenum Press (1983).

2   Allen, S G, and Harlen, F. Sources of exposure to radiofrequency and microwave radiations in the UK. Chilton, NRPB-R144 (1983) (London, HMSO).

3   Durney, C H, Johnson, C C, Barber, P W, Massoudi, H, Iskander, M F, Lords, J L, Ryser, D K, Allen, S J, and Mitchell, J C. Radiofrequency dosimetry handbook (2nd edition). Brooks Airforce Base, Texas, USAF School of Aerospace Medicine, Report SAM-TR-78-22 (1978).

4   Durney, C H, Massoudi, H, and Iskander, M F. Radiofrequency dosimetry handbook (4th edition). Brooks Airforce Base, Texas, USAF School of Aerospace Medicine, Report SAM-TR-85-73 (1986).

5   Dimbylow, P J. The calculation of induced currents and absorbed power in a realistic, heterogeneous model of the lower leg for applied fields from 60 Hz to 30 MHz. *Phys. Med. Biol.,* **33**, No. 12, 1453 (1988).

6   Bernhardt, J H. The establishment of frequency dependent limits for electric and magnetic fields and evaluation of indirect effects. *Radiat. Environ. Biophys.,* **27**, 1 (1988).

7   Dimbylow, P J. Finite-difference time-domain calculations of absorbed power in the ankle for 10–100 MHz plane wave exposure. *IEEE Trans. Biomed. Eng.,* **BME-38**, 423 (1991).

8   IRPA. Guidelines on limits of exposure to radiofrequency electromagnetic fields in the frequency range 100 kHz to 300 GHz. *Health Phys.,* **54**, 115 (1988).

9   NRPB. Guidance as to restrictions on exposures to time varying electromagnetic fields and the 1988 recommendations of the International Non-ionizing Radiation Committee. Chilton, NRPB-GS11 (1989) (London, HMSO).

10 ANSI. Safety levels with respect to human exposure to radiofrequency electromagnetic fields, 300 kHz to 100 GHz. New York, Institute of Electrical and Electronics Engineers, American National Standard C95.1 (1982).

11 IRPA. Interim guidelines on limits of exposure to 50/60 Hz electric and magnetic fields. *Health Phys.,* **58**, 113 (1990).

12 Tell, R A, Mantiply, E D, Durney, C H, and Massoudi, H. Electric and magnetic field intensities and associated induced currents in man in close proximity to a 50 kW AM standard broadcast station. IN Program Abtracts, United States National Committee, International Union of Radio Science, and Bioelectromagnetics Symposium, June 1979, Seattle, Washington (1979).

13 EPRI. *Transmission Line Reference Book 345 kV and Above.* Palo Alto, California, Electrical Power Research Institute (1982).

14 Bowman, R R. Quantifying hazardous electromagnetic fields: Practical considerations. Washington DC, National Bureau of Standards Technical Note 389 (1970).

15 Bowman, R. Some recent developments in the characterisation and measurement of hazardous electromagnetic fields. IN *Biological Effects and Health Hazards of Microwave Radiation.* Proceedings of an International Symposium. Warsaw, Polish Medical Publishers, p 217 (1974).

16 Aslan, E. Broadband isotropic electromagnetic radiation monitor. *IEEE Trans.,* **IM-21**, 411 (1972).

17 Hopfer, S, and Adler, D. An ultra broad-band (200 kHz – 26 GHz) high sensitivity probe. *IEEE Trans.,* **IM-29**, 445 (1980).

18 Aslan, E. An ANSI radiation protection guide conformal probe. *Microwave J.,* April (1983).

19   Tell, R A. Instrumentation for measurement of electromagnetic fields: Equipment, calibrations, and selected applications. IN *Biological Effects and Dosimetry of Non-ionizing Radiation, Radiofrequency and Microwave Energies* (M Grandolfo *et al*, eds). New York, Plenum Press (1983).

20   Bassen, H I, and Smith, G S. Electric field probes — A review. *IEEE Trans.,* **AP-31,** 710 (1983).

21   Smith, G S. Limitations on the size of miniature electric field probes. *IEEE Trans. Microwave Theory Tech.,* **MTT-32,** 594 (1984).

22   Tell, R A. Real time data averaging to determine human RF exposure. IN *Proceeedings 40th Annual Broadcast Engineering Conference,* National Association of Broadcasters, Dallas, Texas (1986).

23   Kaune, W T, Stevens, R G, Callahan, N J, Severson, R K, and Thomas, D B. Residential magnetic and electric fields. *Bioelectromagnetics.* **8,** 315 (1987).

24   Male, J C, Norris, W T, Maddock, B J, and Bonnell, J A. Alternating electric and magnetic fields near electric-power equipment: Are they a health hazard? *J. Radiol. Prot.,* **5,** No. 4, 179 (1985).

25   Deadman, J E, Camus, M, Armstrong, B G, Heroux, P, Cyr, D, Plante, M, and Theriault, G. Occupational and residential 60 Hz electromagnetic fields and high-frequency electric transients: Exposure assessment using a new dosimeter. *J. Am. Ind. Hyg. Assoc.,* **49,** 409 (1988).

26   Bowman, J D, Garabant, E S, Sobel, E, and Peters, J M. Exposures to extremely low frequency (ELF) electromagnetic fields in occupations with elevated leukemia rates. *Appl. Ind. Hyg.,* **3,** No. 6, 189 (1988).

27   Stuchly, M A, Lecuyer, D W, and Mann, R D. Extremely low frequency electromagnetic emissions from video display terminals and other devices. *Health Phys.,* **45,** 713 (1983).

28   Renew, D C, Male, J C, and Maddock, B J. Power frequency magnetic fields: Measurement and exposure assessment. Paris, Cigré, August—September (1990).

29   Gamberale, F, Olsen, B A, Enroth, P, Lindh, T, and Wennberg, A. Acute effects of ELF electromagnetic fields: A field study of linesmen working with 400 kV power lines. *Br. J. Ind. Med.,* **46,** 729 (1989).

30   Stuchly, M A, and Lecuyer, D W. Exposure to electromagnetic fields in arc welding. *Health Phys.,* **56,** No. 3, 297 (1989).

31   Lovsund, P, Oberg, P A, and Nilsson, S E. ELF magnetic fields in electrosteel and welding industries. *Radio Sci.,* **17,** No. 5S, 35S (1982).

32   Stuchly, M A. Human exposure to static and time-varying magnetic fields. *Health Phys.,* **51,** 215 (1986).

33   EPRI. Pilot study of residential power frequency magnetic fields. Palo Alto, California, Electrical Power Research Institute, EPRI- EL-6509 (1989).

34   Preston-Martin, S, Peters, J M, Yu, M C, Garabant, D H, and Bowman, J D. Mylogenous leukemia and electric blanket use. *Bioelectromagnetics,* **9,** 207 (1988).

35   Florig, H K, and Hoburg, J F. Power frequency magnetic fields from electric blankets. *Health Phys.,* **58,** No. 4, 493 (1990).

36   Kavet, R, Silva, J M, and Thornton, D. Magnetic field exposure assessment for adult residents of Maine who live near and far away from overhead transmission lines. *Bioelectromagnetics,* **13,** 35 (1992).

37   Belanger, K, Sachse, K, Hellenbrand, K, Bracken, M, and Leaderer, B. Residential measurement of magnetic field exposure: Variability between rooms. IN *Abstracts, 12th Annual Meeting of the Bioelectromagnetics Society,* San Antonio, Texas (1990).

38   Gauger, J R. Household appliance magnetic field survey. *IEEE Trans. Power Appar. Syst.,* **PAS-104,** No. 9, 2436 (1985).

39   Stuchly, M A, and Lecuyer, D W. Induction heating and operator exposure to electromagnetic fields. *Health Phys.,* **49,** No. 2, 215 (1986).

40   Conover, D L, Murray, W E, Larry, J M, and Johnson, P H. Magnetic field measurements near RF induction heaters. *Bioelectromagnetics,* **7,** 83 (1986).

41   Conover, D. Measurement of electric- and magnetic-field strengths from industrial radiofrequency (6—38 MHz) plastic sealers. *Proc. IEEE,* **68,** 17 (1980).

42   Erikson, A, and Hansson Mild, K. Radio-frequency electromagnetic leakage fields from plastic welding machines. *J. Microwave Power,* **20,** No. 2, 95 (1985).

43   Bini, M, Checcucci, A, Ignesti, A, Millanta, L, Olmi, R, Rubino, N, and Vanni, R. Exposure of workers to intense RF electric fields that leak from plastic sealers. *J. Microwave Power,* **21,** 33 (1986).

44   Chatterjee, I, Hagmann, M J, and Gandhi, O P. An empirical relationship for electromagnetic energy absorption in man for near-field exposure conditions. *IEEE Trans. Microwave Theory Tech.,* **MTT-29,** 11 (1985).

45   Allen, S G, Blackwell, R P, and Unsworth, C. Field intensity measurements, body currents, specific absorption rates and their relevance to operators of dielectric PVC welding machines. IN *Proceedings of BNCE Conference on Heating and Processing,* Cambridge (1986).

46   Gandhi, O P, Chen, J-Y, and Riazi, A. Currents induced in a human being for plane-wave exposure conditions 0—50 MHz and for RF sealers. *IEEE Trans. Biomed. Eng.,* **BME-33,** 8 (1986).

47   Chen, J Y, and Gandhi, O P. RF current induced in an anatomically-based model of a human for plane-wave exposure 20—100 MHz. *Health Phys.,* **57,** 89 (1989).

48   Lambdin, D L. An investigation of energy densities in the vicinity of vehicles with mobile communications equipment and near a hand-held walkie-talkie. Washington DC, Environmental Protection Agency, Technical Note ORP/EAD 79-2 (1978).

49   Tell, R A, and Mantiply, E D. Population exposure to VHF and UHF broadcast radiation in the United States. *Proc. IEEE,* **68,** No. 1, 6 (1980).

50   Balzano, Q, Garay, O, and Steel, F R. Heating of biological tissue in the induction field of VHF portable radio transmitters. *IEEE Trans.,* **VT-27,** 51 (1978).

51   Chatterjee, I, Gu, Y, and Gandhi, O P. Quantification of electromagnetic absorption in humans from body-mounted communications transceivers. *IEEE Trans.,* **VT-34,** 55 (1985).

52   Cleveland, R F, and Athey, T W. Specific absorption rate (SAR) in models of the human head exposed to hand held UHF portable radios. *Bioelectromagnetics,* **10,** 173 (1989).

53   Jokala, K, Aaltonen, J, and Lukkarinen, A. Measurements of electromagnetic emissions from video display terminals at the frequency range from 30 Hz to 1 MHz. *Health Phys.,* **57,** 79 (1989).

54   Tofani, S, and D'Amore, G D. Extremely-low-frequency and very-low-frequency fields emitted by video display units. *Bioelectromagnetics,* **12,** 35 (1991).

55   Kavet, R, and Tell, R A. VDTs: Field levels, epidemiology and laboratory studies. *Health Phys.,* **61,** 47 (1991).

56   British Standard 3456: Part 102:1988. Appliances for heating food by means of microwave energy. London, BSI (1988).

57   HELA. Microwave oven energy leakage — survey. London, Microwaves/radiation data sheet HSE 100/11 (1989).

58   Hankin, N N. The radiofrequency radiation environment: Environmental exposure levels and RF radiation emitting sources. Washington DC, Environmental Protection Agency, Report EPA 520/1-85-014 (1986).

59   Ministry of Defence. Guide to the practical safety aspects of the use of radiofrequency energy. London, Defence Standard 05-74/Issue 1 (1989).

3 Biological Effects of Exposure to Static and Time Varying Electromagnetic Fields and Radiation

INTRODUCTION

1   The biological effects, including the effect on human health, of exposure to electromagnetic fields and radiation up to 300 GHz have been reviewed in detail in four Board reports[1-4]; the three reports describing experimental work are summarised only briefly here, epidemiological studies are described elsewhere in this document. Reference to the original papers that report effects are given in the detailed Board reports and are repeated here only when they bear on the potential carcinogenic effects with which this report is principally concerned. Paragraphs 70–74 provide some concluding remarks on the experimental evidence for a possible association between electromagnetic field exposure and carcinogenesis.

BASIC MECHANISMS OF INTERACTION

2   The photon energy of non-ionising electromagnetic radiation is too small to affect chemical bonding directly; at 300 GHz (the border between microwave and infrared radiation), the photon energy is only about 10^{-3} eV and decreases linearly with decreasing frequency. Covalent bond disruption has an activation energy of 5 eV, and even hydrogen bond disruption has an activation energy of 10^{-1} eV. The electric fields induced in tissue by electromagnetic radiation result in energy absorption due to the polarisation of electrically charged structures and the flow of ions and hence electric current.

Strong field interactions

3   The electric charge phenomena (termed relaxation processes) are frequency dependent, although they do not show sharp resonances because of interactions with adjacent molecules. Biological tissue is characterised by four dispersion (energy absorbing or dissipating) regions, as follows. Alpha dispersion (up to 10 kHz) and beta dispersion (10 kHz — 100 MHz) result from the movement of ions around cell membranes and intracellular structures, and from the capacitative charging of cellular membranes. Smaller contributions result from the relaxation of asymmetrically charged molecules; for example, the contribution from proteins and nucleic acids to the overall absorption of electromagnetic energy is greatest at frequencies between about 1 kHz and 10 MHz. Delta dispersion is caused by the relaxation of water molecules bound to macromolecules and is maximal between 100 MHz and 1 GHz; some contributions are made from smaller amino acids and charged groups in polypeptide chains. Gamma dispersion results from the relaxation of the bulk water in the system and peaks near 20 GHz.

4   In the extremely low frequency (ELF) region, however, ionic conduction processes predominate. The impedance of cell membranes to current flow is high; the flow of current, mainly through the extracellular fluid, induces changes in the electric potential that exists across cell membranes and can, if sufficiently intense, induce conformational changes in voltage sensitive protein 'ion channel gates' such as those in nerve or muscle cells. Changes in ion channel conductivity are clearly associated with the electrical excitability of nerve cells and may initiate or induce changes in electrical activity. It seems reasonable to suppose that other aspects of cell function might also respond to changes in membrane potential, although this is not established; however, any responses associated with increased cellular proliferation would be of particular significance for carcinogenicity. Tissue conductivity increases as frequency increases. Above 100 kHz, cell membranes become progressively short-circuited due to the decrease in their reactance and the ability of electromagnetic radiation to induce electric potentials across the cell membrane decreases.

Weak field interactions

5   The view that very weak fields, such as those encountered in the home, can have biologically significant interactions is controversial. A fundamental difficulty with this concept is that the internally induced electric fields will be so minute that they will be completely masked by thermally generated electrical noise.

6   A number of interaction mechanisms have been proposed in order to account for some of the experimental observations of biological responses to very weak fields, although none has been established experimentally. It has been suggested, for example, that cellular responses to weak ELF magnetic fields may involve an amplification process in which a weak electric field in the extracellular fluid acts as a 'trigger' for the initiation of long-range co-operative events within the cell membrane and that the stored energy resulting from this collective mode of molecular excitation is released through the activation of ion pumps or enzymic reactions within the membrane. Another proposal is that biological responses to weak fields may result from the combined interaction of a 'resonant' ELF frequency and the local geomagnetic field. One suggestion is that kinetic energy could be imparted by a resonant ELF electric or magnetic field to ions moving in a helical path (due to the static magnetic field) through a membrane ion channel; there are, however, a number of biophysical objections to this mechanism. These are avoided in more recent proposals in which it has been suggested that a combination of a weak static field and a resonant time varying field could alter the affinity of ion-binding sites on proteins, thus affecting their biological activity.

7   An important corollary of some of the proposed weak field interaction mechanisms is that it remains possible that biological responses may occur only under certain conditions of exposure. The occurrence of both frequency and amplitude 'windows' has been suggested; resonant interactions imply effects resulting only from exposure to an appropriate combination of ELF and static fields. These proposed mechanisms may have material implications for the possible carcinogenicity of electromagnetic fields. However, it is considered that they are not well established and therefore cannot at present be meaningfully incorporated into the design of large-scale animal or epidemiological studies.

BIOLOGICAL STUDIES

8   The interactions and biological effects of non-ionising radiation differ in different regions of the electromagnetic spectrum and will be discussed under three separate regions.

Static (time invariant) electric and magnetic fields

9   An electric charge is induced on the surface of an object within a static electric field. At a sufficiently high voltage, the air will ionise and become capable of conducting an electric current between, for example, a charged object and a human in good electrical contact with the ground.

10   Magnetic fields can alter nuclear and electron energy levels and spin orientation, and will exert a force on biological molecules. However, magnetic field interactions with atomic nuclei are very weak compared to those with electrons and are likely to be of little biological consequence. Biologically significant interactions with electrons will be those in which the relative spin orientation of electrons available for bond formation can be altered. An effect on chemical reactions involving a radical pair as an intermediate stage in the reaction pathway has been well established in organic chemical reactions at moderate levels of exposure (several millitesla, mT) but has not been clearly demonstrated in biological reactions.

11   Static magnetic fields interact with ionic currents, as a result of the Lorentz forces exerted on moving charge carriers, to produce an electric field. Estimated maximum values generated across the human aorta resulting from the flow of blood in a static field range from about 7 to 16 mV T^{-1}. A static magnetic field will also exert a physical force on a flowing conductor, such as blood, which is proportional to the ionic conduction current and the magnetic flux density. It has been predicted that the net effect of this magnetohydrodynamic interaction will be a drop in aortic blood flow rate with a concomitant increase in pressure; however, this has not been tested experimentally.

Human studies

12   *Electric fields* A static electric field will induce a surface charge on exposed humans, which may be perceived if discharged to an object of different potential. Discharge from a low impedance source, capable of delivering a substantial electric charge, could be fatal. In contrast, a charged, insulated person touching a grounded object would only receive a microshock.

13   *Magnetic fields* Studies of possible effects on circadian rhythms (daily fluctuations in metabolic and physiological processes) are not normally considered in an investigation of toxic effects. However, it is conceivable that adverse effects might influence general well being, although these rhythms tend to be strongly reinforced by daily time cues such as the light/dark cycle, eating and sleeping. Studies of possible static magnetic field effects on volunteers show that chronic exposure to fields of 0.15 mT had no effect on human circadian rhythms, nor did the exposure to fields of up to 0.15 T for up to 1 h have any effect on mental performance.

14   Higher flux densities are routinely encountered in the use of magnetic resonance imaging (MRI) and spectroscopy (MRS) units for clinical diagnosis; patients and volunteers may be exposed to flux densities of up to 2.5 T (approximately 50 000 times the natural geomagnetic field) or even up to 4 T in a few experimental systems. Several experiments report that body temperature, heart rate and blood pressure were unaffected by acute exposure to fields up to about 1.5 T, although one study reported a slight drop in heart rate in humans exposed to 2 T. Another study reported that workers experienced vertigo and nausea during rapid head movement in a 4 T field; these responses did not occur in subjects lying stationary within the field.

Animal studies

15 *Electric fields* No consistent effects on rodent behaviour have been found after exposure to up to 12 kV m^{-1}. Animal studies do not indicate any adverse effect of exposure to fields of up to 340 kV m^{-1} on haematology or on reproduction and prenatal and postnatal survival.

16 *Magnetic fields* Carefully conducted experiments have failed to find any evidence of an effect of chronic exposure up to about 1.5 T on circadian rhythms or on the spontaneous and learned behaviour of rodents. Experiments with mammals, including two primate species, found no effect on cardiac function of exposure to fields of less than about 2 T. A temporary increase in sinus arrhythmia and decrease in heart rate were observed in one experiment in which squirrel monkeys were acutely exposed to fields mainly between 4 and 7 T, although the data did not allow a threshold to be identified.

17 Exposures to more intense static magnetic fields (up to 9.7 T) have been reported to disrupt animal behaviour. Two studies report that the performance of learned (operant) tasks by squirrel monkeys was reduced during exposure to static fields in excess of about 4.6 T. The evidence from studies of nervous system responses is equivocal. Changes in the electroencephalogram of squirrel monkeys during exposure to between 2 and 9 T were reported in one study, although these responses could be artifacts resulting from muscle activity.

18 There is no unequivocal evidence from animal studies that chronic exposure to static magnetic fields of 1—2 T over days to years has any adverse effect on body weight, haematological profile or immunological response. Experimentally induced changes in the orientation of static magnetic fields at around geomagnetic flux densities have been reported to have variable effects on nocturnal melatonin activity in rodents: more intense fields (of up to 2 T) have had no effect on other hormone levels investigated. Exposure to about 1 T *in vitro* has had no significant effect on prenatal or postnatal development. Exposure to fields of up to about 1 T appears to affect neither dominant lethal mutation frequency in male germ cells irradiated *in vivo*, nor the frequency of chromosome aberrations and sister chromatid exchanges in cells exposed *in vivo* or *in vitro*. Tumour growth in mice was unaffected by exposure to fields of up to about 1 T[5,6], as was the survival time of mice treated with the carcinogen methylcholanthrene[7].

Conclusions

19 (1) There is little evidence of any adverse effect of static electric fields on human health except possibly those associated with surface charge.

(2) There is no evidence of any adverse effect on human health due to short-term exposure to static magnetic fields of up to 2 T.

(3) Static magnetic fields of up to at least 1 T do not appear to be mutagenic, nor does tumour progression or promotion appear to be affected by exposure to such fields; however, few studies have been carried out.

(4) There are additional areas of biological investigation, particularly the possible effects of exposure on enzyme reactions involving radical intermediate pairs, in which effects of static magnetic fields have been described and which may, in principle, have health implications but these have yet to be established.

Electric and magnetic fields up to 100 kHz

20   Extremely low frequency electric fields induce time varying electric charges on the surface of the body which are mainly dependent on the shape of the body and its location and orientation relative to the ground. The electrostatic effects of surface charge, such as hair vibration resulting from time varying forces exerted on body hair, produce perceptible effects on the body surface. Electric currents or spark discharges result from contact or close proximity between grounded and ungrounded bodies in an ELF electric field.

21   Electric fields and currents are induced inside the body as a result of time variation of the induced surface charge density and are linearly dependent on frequency. In the ELF range, the variation is so slow that the currents and fields generated inside the body are very small. Estimates show that the internal electric fields are generally less than about 10^{-7} of the field outside the body and probably never exceed about 10^{-4} of the external field. The total current passing through any section of the body depends only on the surface charge; the induced current density distribution depends on the electrical properties of tissues but in general varies inversely with body cross-section and may be relatively high in the neck and ankles of humans.

22   Time varying magnetic fields exert a force on charged particles such as ions or asymmetrically charged molecules. Circulating electric currents are induced in animals and humans in such a way that the largest current densities tend to be induced in peripheral tissues, decreasing in magnitude towards the centre of the body, although the actual distribution of current will be affected by tissue inhomogeneity. The magnitude of the induced current density also depends on body size and orientation and increases linearly with increasing frequency.

Human studies

23   *Electric fields*   Extremely low frequency electric fields are perceptible if they are sufficiently intense. For adults, 10% can perceive 50–60 Hz fields of less than 10–15 kV m^{-1}; 5% can detect fields as low as 3–5 kV m^{-1}, levels similar to those found under some high voltage power lines. These effects become annoying at around 15–20 kV m^{-1}. The threshold for the perception of spark discharges by 10% of a group of volunteers has been reported to be 0.6–1.5 kV m^{-1} at 50–60 Hz, with a threshold for annoyance of about 2–3.5 kV m^{-1}.

24   Most available evidence suggests that simple measures of nervous system function in humans are unaffected by exposure to fields up to at least 20 kV m^{-1}, although one well-conducted study reported slight changes in heart rate and electroencephalogram recordings in subjects exposed to 60 Hz fields of only 9 kV m^{-1}. The exposure of volunteers to a simulated 50 Hz electric field of 36 kV m^{-1}, applied via electrodes in an attempt to circumvent cutaneous perception of the field, resulted in

altered levels of arousal and response latencies for some tests of reasoning in one out of two trials; however, the experimental design rendered the results difficult to interpret. Peak induced current density in the brain was estimated to be $4-10$ mA m^{-2}.

25   One extensive but unreplicated study suggests that very low level (2.5 V m^{-1}) 10 Hz, electric fields can affect the circadian rhythms of volunteers living in environments artificially isolated from normal temporal cues such as light/dark cycles.

26   No consistent effect on haematology and blood biochemistry has been found in human subjects exposed to $50-60$ Hz fields of up to 20 kV m^{-1}.

27   *Magnetic fields*   Most evidence suggests that humans cannot perceive ELF magnetic fields of up to about $1-5$ mT. Above this level it is possible to induce faint flickering visual sensations — magnetic phospenes — which are thought to result from an effect of induced electric current on the activity of excitable cells in the retina. The threshold is frequency dependent, being minimal ($5-10$ mT) at around 20 Hz and increasing to about 15 mT at $50-60$ Hz. Volunteers exposed to 50 Hz magnetic fields above 60 mT complained of headaches. At higher frequencies (about 1 kHz), rapidly changing magnetic fields of about 8 mT have been reported as stimulating nerve endings or muscles in superficial tissues.

28   Few effects have been reported at power frequency magnetic fields below 1 mT. One unreplicated study reported a significant decrement in the performance of mental arithmetic and an improvement in a short-term memory task during exposure of volunteers to 45 Hz fields of 0.1 mT, returning to control values after exposure. No field-related changes in a number of haematological and serum chemistry parameters were observed in volunteers exposed to 45 Hz fields of 0.1 mT for up to about 1 day, except for elevated serum triglyceride levels; these were partly ascribed to a number of confounding influences.

Animal studies

29   *Electric fields*   There is no clear, unequivocal, consistently replicated evidence of an effect of electric field exposure on animal nervous system responses, although some studies report induced changes at field levels well above perceptual thresholds. Changes have been reported in the electroencephalogram of Guinea-pigs exposed to 60 Hz fields of 100 kV m^{-1}, in the evoked potentials of primates exposed to 60 Hz fields of $10-30$ kV m^{-1}, and in synaptic transmission in rats after exposure to 100 kV m^{-1} at 60 Hz. In addition, one study reported changes in the levels of neurotransmitter metabolites in the cerebrospinal fluid of primates chronically exposed to 60 Hz fields at $3-30$ kV m^{-1}.

30   The evidence from most animal studies would support a lack of overall effect of electric fields of up to 30 kV m^{-1} on the performance of learned tasks by primates, although response latencies to some tasks decreased. Some studies have reported transient arousal responses and changes in activity in rodents exposed to fields of up to 100 kV m^{-1} and transient changes in the social and grooming behaviour of baboons exposed to up to 30 kV m^{-1}. However, such effects may be consistent with the initial distraction cause by cutaneous stimulation.

31   Evidence from animal studies supports an effect on various circadian rhythms of chronic exposure to intense electric fields (about $40-100$ kV m^{-1} in rodents and $25-40$ kV m^{-1} in primates) but in the absence of other time cues. Several studies implicated changes to the diurnal secretion of melatonin from the pineal body as a possible mechanism; a reduction of the natural night-time peak in the production of melatonin by the pineal gland has been reported in rats exposed for more than 3 weeks in the presence of normal light/dark cycles to unperturbed 60 Hz electric fields of 60 and 65 kV m^{-1} (a value as low as about 1.5–2 kV m^{-1}, determined retrospectively after equipment failure, has yet to be confirmed). However, it is worth noting in this context that the diurnal rhythm of metatonin secretion is inhibited by constant illumination; in addition, the night-time peak in melatonin production can also be reduced by transient night-time illumination.

32   Most recent, well-conducted experiments have shown no effect on the immune response of rodents exposed to 50–60 Hz fields of up to 130 kV m^{-1}. Similarly, no effects have been seen on circulating endocrine levels in rodents exposed to 60 Hz electric fields of up to 100 kV m^{-1} when confounding variables have been eliminated.

33   Possible effects of electric field exposure on reproduction and development have been investigated in a number of large, carefully conducted studies in which rodents or miniature swine have been exposed to 60 Hz fields as high as 130 kV m^{-1}. There appear to be no effects of exposure to such high fields on male fertility or on reproductive performance, nor were any consistent effects on development established. Some statistically significant changes in malformation incidence were reported but either were not reproducible in replicate experiments or the incidence varied widely between sham groups but was, overall, of a similar range to that in the exposed groups. One recent, but unreplicated, study reported that learning was significantly impaired in adult rats exposed prenatally and postnatally to 60 Hz electric fields of up to 30 kV m^{-1} and concomitant magnetic fields of up to 0.1 mT.

34   In general, no mutagenic effects of ELF electric or magnetic fields have been seen. Exposure to 20 kV m^{-1} at 50 Hz failed to increase the frequency of dominant lethal mutations in male mice; nor did exposure to 60 Hz electric fields of up to 50 kV m^{-1} combined with magnetic fields of up to 1 mT affect the frequency of sister chromatid exchanges in the bone marrow cells of mice.

35   The lack of effect on chromosome structure has suggested that if electromagnetic fields have a role in carcinogenesis, they are more likely to act as promoters than as initiators, enhancing cancer cell proliferation rather than causing the initial transformation. Field-induced changes in melatonin secretion have been suggested as a possible contributory factor in the development particularly of mammary (breast) cancer[8]. Some experimental data suggest that melatonin has the properties of an endogenous anti-tumour factor[9]; the application of this hormone in physiological concentrations was reported to inhibit the growth of mammary tumour cell lines[10] and reduce the incidence of chemically induced mammary cancer in rats[11,12]. Two recent studies[13,14] indicate that the exposure of female rats to 60 Hz electric fields of 40 kV m^{-1} for 18 or 23 weeks did not affect the number of rats with chemically induced mammary tumours compared to controls but only marginally increased the number of tumours per tumour-bearing rat. It is possible, however, that the experimental protocol was not optimal for this proposed effect; it may be premature to discount this hypothesis without further investigation.

36   *Magnetic fields* Studies of effects on animal behaviour have yielded equivocal results; in general, reported effects have not been replicated in well-conducted and carefully controlled studies.

37   Much experimental evidence suggests a lack of effect on haematology and blood chemistry in rodents and primates exposed to 15—60 Hz fields in the range of 10—100 mT. No consistent effect of exposure has been seen on the immune response of rodents, although few studies have been carried out.

38   A number of studies have been carried out of the possible teratogenic effects of exposure to ELF magnetic fields. Several groups have described abnormal development, particularly at the head end, of chick embryos exposed to pulsed or sinusoidal magnetic fields greater than 1.2 µT at frequencies between 10 and 1000 Hz. In contrast, other groups have reported a lack of statistically significant effects after the exposure of chick embryos to pulsed or sawtooth magnetic fields at frequencies of 100 Hz up to 20 kHz (typical of visual display units). A large-scale, carefully conducted study which attempted to define the response of chick embryos to low level, low frequency fields using six replicate experiments failed to provide clear evidence of a response; overall, the results indicated a statistically significant increase in malformations in the exposed group, but there were significant differences between the results of the replicate studies.

39   Several studies have examined the effects on mammalian development of exposure to these low level ELF fields; however, most results are negative when malformation incidence is analysed by litter. Several studies have reported a lack of effect of exposure of pregnant mice or rats to 18—20 kHz asymmetrical 'sawtooth' magnetic fields at up to 200 µT; variable effects on implantation rate were reported. One recent study failed to find any developmental effects in rat fetuses after exposure to 50 Hz magnetic fields of 15 mT. It would seem at present that it is unlikely that mammalian development will be affected by exposure to magnetic fields, but the relevant research is still at a preliminary stage.

40   Two studies have looked at the effect of magnetic fields on tumour progression. One study described a lack of effect of exposure to 60 Hz magnetic fields of up to 500 µT on the progression of leukaemia, induced by the injection of leukaemic cells, in mice[15]; another study found that mice with spontaneous mammary tumours periodically exposed at up to 6 mT at frequencies of up to 460 Hz lived longer and had less metastatic invasion than controls[16].

Electrophysiological considerations

41   There is a well-established literature describing the effects of electric currents, usually applied via external electrodes, on excitable tissue. Threshold current densities for direct nerve or muscle stimulation are thought to be about 1—10 A m^{-2} between about 1 and 1000 Hz. Such current densities are thought to have been induced in the peripheral tissues of volunteers who experienced sensation or muscle twitches when exposed to 1—1.5 kHz magnetic fields of about 8 mT. Current densities unable to stimulate excitable tissue directly may nevertheless affect electrical activity. Conventional electrophysiological studies have shown that current densities of between about 100 and 1000 mA m^{-2} can modulate post-synaptic activity in central nervous tissue. A conservative estimate of current density threshold for this effect of 10 mA m^{-2} can be derived from the human phosphene response data and from studies of the responses of molluscan pacemaker cells to directly applied electric fields. In this context, however, it should be noted that current densities of up to 1 mA m^{-2} circulate within body tissue as a result of the endogenous electrical activity of nerves and muscles and may reach 10 mA m^{-2} in the heart during contraction.

Cellular studies

42   Many *in-vitro* studies have involved exposure to magnetic fields or the direct application of electric currents, often to human or rodent tumour cell cultures. Most report a lack of effect of directly applied electric fields, or magnetic fields, on chromosome aberration, sister chromatid exchange frequency or point mutation frequency in human lymphocytes or Chinese hamster ovary (CHO) cells.

43   The possibility that electromagnetic fields might stimulate cell proliferation has also been examined. Two studies report transient changes in the activity of ornithine decarboxylase, an enzyme involved in cellular proliferation, in human lymphoma cells[17] and mouse C3H10T½ fibroblasts[18] exposed to 60 Hz electric fields of 10 mV m^{-1} or 1 V m^{-1} (5 and 500 mA m^{-2}, assuming a conductivity of 0.5 S m^{-1}) applied directly to the preparation. Several studies[19–23] by one group describe enhanced DNA transcription, indicating elevated gene expression, and altered levels of protein synthesis in dipteran (fly) salivary glands after exposure to 1–72 Hz pulsed and sinusoidal magnetic fields of about 0.5–3.5 mT. However, the evidence for direct effects on cell proliferation, assayed by examination of the colony-forming ability of human colon cancer cells, has proved equivocal[24–27].

44   Studies of the mechanisms of interaction of ELF electric fields with tissues are valuable in suggesting basic dose–response relationships. Two principal research groups have identified changes in the exchange of $^{45}Ca^{2+}$ in isolated chick brain in response to very weak external electric fields at some frequencies between about 1 and 400 Hz and at some field strengths between 1 and 100 V m^{-1}. These, and other, data challenge the conventional view that the magnitude of an effect increases simply with increasing field strength and exposure duration.

Conclusions

45 (1) People can perceive the effects of surface charge induced on their bodies by low frequency electric fields; thresholds for annoyance are 15–20 kV m^{-1} for hair vibration, and as low as about 2–3.5 kV m^{-1} for microshocks to grounded objects.

      (2) It can be conservatively estimated that, in the frequency range 1–1000 Hz, induced current densities greater than about 10 mA m^{-2} may affect electrically excitable cells, particularly those in the central nervous system. A number of metabolic changes in various cell lines have been reported at current densities mostly between 10 and 1000 mA m^{-2}; however, these responses are not well established.

      (3) Time varying electromagnetic fields up to 100 kHz (including power frequencies) are not mutagenic and are therefore unlikely to initiate cancers. The experimental evidence from animal studies for an effect of ELF electric fields on tumour promotion or progression is marginal; two studies reported a lack of effect on tumour progression of exposure to ELF magnetic fields. Prolonged exposure to electric fields has been reported to decrease the night-time peak in the production and secretion of melatonin, a possible inhibitor of tumour growth,

particularly of mammary tumours. The prolonged 60 Hz electric field exposure of rats resulted in only a marginal increase in the incidence of chemically induced mammary tumours; however, the experimental conditions may not have been optimal. The changes induced in metabolic endpoints associated with cell proliferation, such as transcription, are not in themselves sufficient to imply promotional activity. Nevertheless, these studies are of sufficient importance to warrant further investigation (see Chapter 9).

(4) There are additional areas of biological investigation in which effects of electric and magnetic fields up to 100 kHz have been described which may have health implications but which are not well understood. These areas include possible effects of exposure on circadian rhythms and on prenatal and postnatal development. In addition, there remain uncertainties about low level interaction mechanisms and appropriate dose—response relationships.

Radiofrequency effects above 100 kHz (including microwaves)

46   In general, as frequencies increase, power absorption per unit mass of tissue increases and penetration decreases. However, the coupling of radiofrequency (RF) and microwave radiation to the body depends on the orientation relative to the field and on body size relative to the wavelength. Coupling is maximal when the long axis of the body is oriented parallel to the electric field and when the body length is similar to the wavelength. Thus maximum (resonant) absorption conditions occur at around 40 MHz for an average (electrically grounded) man, at around 600—700 MHz for a rat and at around 2.4—2.6 GHz for a mouse. When the radiation wavelength is smaller than the overall dimensions of the body, the reflection and refraction of radiation at the interface of materials of different electrical properties can result in localised 'hot spots'. These can occur within the body at frequencies near body resonance, or within parts of the body such as the head at higher frequencies, up to about 2—3 GHz. At frequencies greater than about 10 GHz, absorption is largely confined to the skin.

Human studies

47   A major effect of exposure to RF frequencies above 100 kHz is heating. It seems probable that healthy people can tolerate short-term (minutes—hours) rises in body temperature by up to about 1 °C. This rise is well below the maximum tolerable increase of about 2°C but nevertheless represents a significant thermal load. It can be conservatively estimated from the evidence derived from theoretical calculations and from thermoregulatory responses of humans that a specific absorption rate (SAR) of 1 W kg^{-1}, up to 4 W kg^{-1} for short periods, will result in a rise in body temperature of less than 1 °C in healthy subjects at rest in light clothing and in moderate environmental conditions. Sweating and an increase in heart rate have been seen in resting volunteers in controlled environments in response to whole body SARs in the upper part of this range after exposure for 20 min. However, the total heat load of an exposed person represents the sum of SAR resulting from RF or microwave heating and the rate of metabolic heat production, which increases during physical work. Thus, adverse environmental conditions and moderate physical exercise will reduce the tolerable level of SAR. In addition, people under medication or with clinical conditions which compromise thermoregulation will be more sensitive to RF or microwave exposure.

48   The absorption of RF and microwave radiation can be detected by temperature sensitive receptors in the skin. Power densities of around 300 W m^{-2} at 3 GHz have been detected experimentally during exposure for 10 s; higher frequencies applied for similar lengths of time have been detected at lower power densities because of their greater absorption by the skin. However, in general, it is not possible to give specific thresholds of perception because of their dependence not only on RF or microwave frequency but also on exposure duration and on the part of the body and the area exposed.

49   People with normal hearing have perceived pulse-modulated RF and microwave radiation between about 200 MHz and 6.5 GHz; the sound has been variously described as a buzzing, clicking, hissing or popping noise, depending on modulation characteristics. It seems most likely that the sound results from the thermoelastic expansion of brain tissue following a small but rapid increase in temperature on the absorption of the incident energy. The perception threshold for pulses shorter than 30 μs depends on the energy density per pulse and has been estimated as about 400 mJ m^{-2}, corresponding to an estimated specific energy density in the head of about 16 mJ kg^{-1}. However, a reduction in ambient noise may reduce this to about 10 mJ kg^{-1}.

Animal and cellular studies

50   Animals use various physiological and behavioural mechanisms in order to regulate body temperature. These include altered rates of metabolic heat production, food intake, activity, the vasodilation or constriction of superficial blood vessels and the behavioural selection of appropriate ambient temperatures. Thresholds for such responses have been reported in rodents and primates between about 0.3 and 5 W kg^{-1}. In addition, exposure to frequencies resulting in power absorption in the deeper tissues of the body seems to result in less efficient thermoregulatory performance, probably because of the less effective stimulation of temperature receptors in the skin.

51   Other behavioural responses may be affected by increased heat loads. The performance of learned tasks seems particularly sensitive; thresholds for decreased performance in both rats and primates have been reported as lying between 2.5 and 8 W kg^{-1}; concomitant rises in rectal temperature were around 1 °C. The acquisition of a learned task appears more sensitive to disruption than performance but the experimental data were sometimes variable and inconsistent.

52   Some nervous system responses to very intense, pulsed microwave or RF radiation may be related to microwave hearing, although this is not well established. Exposure to very intense pulsed RF radiation has been reported to suppress the startle response and evoke body movements in conscious mice. Specific absorptions per pulse were 200 mJ kg^{-1} (for 1 μs pulses) for suppression of the startle response and 200 J kg^{-1} (for 10 μs pulses) for evoked body movement. The specific energy per pulse for both effects is several orders of magnitude greater than the auditory threshold for pulsed RF (about 1 mJ kg^{-1} in rats).

53   Other low level effects have been reported which are more difficult to interpret. Exposure to low levels of pulsed or continuous wave microwave or RF radiation at SARs as low as 0.46 W kg^{-1} has been reported to affect neurotransmitter metabolism and the concentration of receptors involved in stress and anxiety responses in different parts of the rat brain. Exposure to very low levels of amplitude-modulated RF or microwave radiation, too low to involve heating, has been reported by several groups to alter brain activity in cats and rabbits (measured using electroencephalography) and to affect calcium ion mobility in the cat cortex *in vivo* and in chick brain tissue *in vitro*. Effective SARs *in vitro* were less than 0.01 W kg^{-1}. These changes in calcium ion mobility have not been easy to corroborate; two groups have failed to observe these effects in similar studies.

54   It has been shown that microwave or RF exposure can modify the action of drugs whose effectiveness can be altered by heat-induced changes in body physiology. Exposure of mice and rabbits at SARs sufficient to raise body temperatures by at least 1 °C significantly reduced barbiturate-induced sleeping time, possibly by increasing the rate of redistribution of the drug. Altered permeability of the blood—brain barrier might well affect the action of psychoactive drugs. The acute exposure of conscious rats to microwave radiation at 13 W kg^{-1}, sufficient to increase brain temperature above 40 °C, altered levels of tracer material within the brain; however, these may have resulted, at least in part, from changes in renal clearance and cerebral blood volume. In severely hyperthermic animals there is some evidence for a decrease in permeability or vesicular transport across the blood—brain barrier. In contrast, the reported effects of low level microwave or RF exposure on the influence of various neuroactive drugs, such as tranquillisers or stimulants, on the electrical activity of the brain are variable and unclear.

55   Endocrine responses to acute microwave exposure are generally consistent with responses to non-specific stressors such as heat. The acute exposure of primates to microwaves or RF at SARs of 3—4 W kg^{-1}, sufficient to raise rectal temperature by 1—2 °C, resulted in increased plasma cortisol levels. Similar effects have been reported in rats. The effect seems to be mediated via the hypothalamus rather than by a direct effect on the adrenal glands and can be influenced by the natural circadian rhythm of these hormone levels. The hypothalamus also controls the secretion of growth hormone and thyroxin; stressful stimuli are known to depress circulating plasma levels of both hormones in rodents. Both have been depressed in rodents exposed at SARs of 4—5 W kg^{-1}; however, no effect has been seen in primates after exposure at similar SARs.

56   A large number of studies of effects of microwave and RF radiation on haemopoietic tissues and immune function have been carried out but results are not always clear; many reports have yielded conflicting data. However, changes that have been reported are usually transient and result from acute, thermally significant exposures. Several authors have reported a decrease in peripheral lymphocyte count and an increase in the neutrophil count in mice and rats exposed at 5—13 W kg^{-1} and 1.5—3 W kg^{-1}, respectively, sufficient under the particular experimental conditions used to raise rectal temperatures about 1 °C or so; the evidence suggests that this is probably a stress-mediated response. In contrast, the chronic exposure of rats for most of their lifetime to up to 0.4 W kg^{-1} had no effect on any haematological parameter.

57   The results of studies of the effects of microwave or RF exposure on leucocyte function are more varied. Several recent studies report changes in natural killer cell and macrophage activity after the acute exposure of hamsters at SARs of about

13 W kg^{-1} or mice at SARs of around 21 W kg^{-1}; rectal temperatures rose by several degrees. The exposure of mice and hamsters, respectively, at 5 and 8 W kg^{-1} and above has been associated with an increase in the primary antibody response of B-lymphocytes. However, the chronic exposure of rats for most of their lifetime at up to 0.4 W kg^{-1} had no effect on a number of immunological responses, except for a transient change in the response of B- and T-lymphocytes to specific mitogens after exposure for 13 months. There have been several *in-vitro* studies of effects on haemopoietic tissues and immune function; no clear pattern of response emerges.

58   Some individual tissues may be particularly sensitive to the heating effects of microwave or RF radiation. The lens of the eye is regarded as potentially sensitive because of its lack of a blood supply (and consequent limited cooling ability) and its tendency to accumulate damage and cellular debris. High local temperatures induced by exposure of the head to microwaves have been shown by many authors to induce cataracts (opacities) in the lens of anaesthetised rabbits; primate eyes, however, seem less susceptible. The most effective frequencies appear to lie between about 1 and 10 GHz. The threshold temperature in the lens for cataract induction for prolonged (100–200 min) exposure is between about 41 and 43 °C; the corresponding local SAR is about 100–140 W kg^{-1}.

59   Effects have also been reported in eye tissue after exposure at lower SARs. Recent, well-conducted studies by one group of workers suggest that the retina, iris and corneal endothelium of anaesthetised primates are susceptible to low level microwave irradiation, particularly to pulsed radiation. Localised threshold SARs for various degenerative changes of 2.6 W kg^{-1}, corresponding to a specific energy per pulse (for 10 μs pulses) of 26 mJ kg^{-1}, to as low as 0.26 W kg^{-1} (a specific energy of 2.6 mJ kg^{-1}) after the application of timolol maleate, have been reported. Confirmation of these effects by other groups is clearly important.

60   The testis is also regarded as heat sensitive. Testicular temperatures are normally several degrees celsius below body temperature, and it has been known for some time that male germ cells, particularly those undergoing meiosis (rather than the recycling stem cell population) are adversely affected by elevated temperatures. Two studies reported that chronic exposure at about 6 W kg^{-1} may have resulted in transient infertility in male rats; rectal or testicular temperatures rose by about 1.5–3.5 °C during exposure. This may be the minimum exposure required to cause a slight loss of male fertility in rats.

61   Exposure to RF or microwave radiation sufficient to induce a significant rise in maternal body temperature is teratogenic. In rats, acute exposure at 11 W kg^{-1}, raising maternal temperatues to 43 °C, was sufficient to induce embryo and fetal death and developmental abnormalities; chronic exposure at 6–7 W kg^{-1}, usually raising maternal temperatures to 39–41 °C, was reported to induce growth retardation and subtle behavioural changes postnatally. In general, exposure at less than 4 W kg^{-1} had no effect. A similar pattern of response was seen in mice but at higher SARs. In addition, one study reported that exposure of mice at 4–5 W kg^{-1} had no direct effect, but increased the effectiveness of a known chemical teratogen.

62   Much experimental evidence suggests that acute or chronic exposure to microwave radiation does not result in an increase in mutation or chromosome aberration frequency when temperatures are maintained within physiological limits. The lack of clear evidence for a mutagenic effect of microwave and RF radiation suggests that these frequencies of electromagnetic radiation are unlikely to be directly carcinogenic. Several long-term studies, in which some biological endpoints relevant to carcinogenesis were examined, have been carried out; however, the early studies[28-31] suffered from insufficient dosimetry, poor histopathology or inadequate follow-up.

63   More recently, an extensive, well-conducted investigation has been carried out[32] on 100 Sprague Dawley rats chronically exposed from 2 to up to 27 months of age to low level pulsed microwave radiation at SARs of up to 0.4 W kg^{-1}; a further 100 rats were sham exposed. As part of this study, the longevity, cause of death and the frequency and site of neoplastic and non-neoplastic lesions were determined[33]. Some animals were sacrificed during the period of exposure, but most animals died spontaneously during the course of the experiment. In each case, a full histopathological analysis was carried out and the age at death noted.

64   An initial analysis of all neoplastic lesions, taking into account age at death, treatment, mode of death and organ, was abandoned due to the sparsity of data. Separate analyses were carried out of the incidence of benign and primary malignancies; metastatic lesions were reported as occurring too seldom for meaningful analysis. The total number of benign tumours of the adrenal medulla (pheochromocytomas) was higher in the exposed group compared to the control group, although not particularly higher than that reported elsewhere for this strain of rat. The authors carried out an analysis of the incidence of all benign neoplasms at death, irrespective of site or mode of death but taking into account age at death and treatment. There was no significant difference between groups; however, the data could be analysed further, taking into account the additional factors described above. The authors reported that no single type of malignant tumour was enhanced by exposure; overall, the incidence of primary malignancies was similar to that reported elsewhere in Sprague Dawley rats. If the incidence of primary malignant lesions were pooled without regard to site or mode of death, the exposed group had a significantly higher incidence compared to the control group. Further analysis suggested that primary malignancies occurred earlier in the exposed group compared to the sham-exposed group.

65   These data are intriguing but do not provide clear evidence of an increase in tumour incidence as a result of exposure to microwaves. The data were analysed without taking into account the type and site of the neoplasm, nor was mode of death incorporated into the analysis. In addition, the incidence of benign neoplasms did not appear enhanced in the exposed group compared to controls; nor was any particular type of neoplasm in the exposed group significantly elevated compared to values reported elsewhere in stock rats of this strain. However, the data could be subjected to a more comprehensive analysis.

66   Another study[34,35] reported that the chronic microwave exposure of mice at 2–8 W kg^{-1} resulted in an SAR-dependent increase in the progression or development of spontaneous (mammary) or chemically induced (skin) tumours. Body temperatures were not raised but the authors suggest a possibility of localised heating at the highest

level of exposure. A further experiment[36] showed that exposure at 4–5 W kg^{-1} followed by the application of a 'sub-carcinogenic' dose of a carcinogen to the skin, a procedure repeated daily, eventually resulted in a three-fold increase in the numbers of skin tumours appearing.

67   *In-vitro* studies have also implied a role for microwave exposure in cancer induction. One study[37] reported enhanced transformation rates in C3H10T½ cells exposed to combined amplitude-modulated microwave radiation (4.4 W kg^{-1}) and X-rays (followed by treatment with the chemical promoter TPA) compared to cells exposed only to X-rays and TPA. A further study[38] reported similar levels of enhanced transformation rates after exposure to microwaves and/or X-rays (1.5 Gy), followed by treatment with the promoter. More recently, it was reported[39] that microwave radiation at SARs between 0.1 and 4.4 W kg^{-1} followed by TPA treatment resulted in a dose-dependent effect on the induction of transformation; in addition, microwave exposure slightly enhanced the effects of X-irradiation and TPA on transformation rate. The results of these studies of the chromosomally abnormal C3H10T½ cells are important but their implications for carcinogenesis *in vivo* are not clear; transformation studies tend to be susceptible to a variety of experimental confounding factors.

68   Other studies[40,41] have reported evidence of an effect of low level, amplitude-modulated microwave radiation on intracellular levels of ornithine decarboxylase, an enzyme involved in tumour promotion. Changes in the levels of this enzyme are not necessarily indicative of promotion or cell transformation, but are of sufficient importance to warrant further investigation.

Conclusions

69 (1) Many of the biological effects of acute exposure to RF radiation above about 100 kHz are consistent with responses to induced heating, resulting either in responses to rises in tissue or body temperature of about 1 °C or more, or in responses for minimising the total heat load. It seems probable that healthy people can tolerate short-term rises in body temperature by up to about 1 °C; some people are less heat tolerant, or are compromised with respect to their thermoregulatory ability. It can be conservatively estimated that temperature rises below 1 °C will be induced in people at rest in moderate environments at SARs of 1 W kg^{-1} up to 4 W kg^{-1} for short periods. High ambient temperatures, physical exercise and other factors will reduce the tolerable level of SAR.

     (2) There is generally less information concerning responses to localised heating resulting from SAR 'hot spots', although thresholds for some effects, such as cataracts, have been identified, particularly in response to acute exposure.

     (3) The evidence suggests that RF and microwave radiation is not mutagenic and is therefore unlikely to initiate cancers. The evidence for a co-carcinogenic effect or an effect on tumour promotion or progression is not convincing but is nevertheless sufficient to justify further investigation (see Chapter 9). One large-scale study reported an increase in the number of primary malignancies in 100 rats exposed for most of their lives to microwave radiation at SARs of up to 0.4 W kg^{-1} when compared to sham-exposed animals, but not when compared to other published frequencies for the same strain of animals; there are other

inconsistencies in the data. The chronic exposure of mice at much higher SARs (2—8 W kg^{-1}), possibly causing some localised heating, resulted in an increase in the progression of spontaneous or chemically induced tumours. Studies of mouse C3H10T½ cells exposed to microwaves at 0.1—4.4 W kg^{-1} followed by TPA treatment revealed a dose-dependent increase in neoplastic transformation rate; however, the results from these chromosomally abnormal cells cannot be directly extrapolated to carcinogenesis *in vivo.*

(4)   There are other areas of biological study in which effects of RF and microwave radiation above 100 kHz have been described, which may have health implications, but which are not well understood. These areas include possible adverse effects of exposure to pulsed radiation. In addition, there remain uncertainties about possible low level interaction mechanisms and dose—response relationships, particularly in relation to amplitude-modulated RF and microwave radiation.

OVERALL SUMMARY AND CONCLUSIONS

70   Experimental studies on the biological effects of exposure to electromagnetic fields have yet to provide unequivocal evidence of any whole animal, cellular or molecular sequelae that are suggestive of a clearly defined role for electromagnetic fields in carcinogenic processes. While individual studies purport to show biological effects that may be linked directly or indirectly to cancer induction, the literature contains many conflicting observations and, in some cases, positive findings from experimentally limited studies.

71   At the fundamental level, evidence continues to accumulate in support of a multistep cellular mechanism for carcinogenesis with the earliest (initiating) cellular event being specific gene or chromosomal mutations in appropriate target cells in tissue[42,43]. Thus, for many directly acting physical and chemical agents, carcinogenicity may be reasonably predicted on the basis of cellular studies which show such agents to act on DNA and, through this, to have the capacity to induce cancer-initiating gene and chromosomal mutations. In this context, perhaps the most informative data on electromagnetic field exposure are those showing that, in the main, exposure under a wide range of conditions does not induce such cell mutations.

72   If, as these data imply, electromagnetic fields do not possess direct tumorigenic activity then conventional large-scale animal carcinogenesis studies may not be sufficiently informative.

73   The multistep process of carcinogenesis may be influenced by a wide range of physical and chemical agents, some of which are not overtly genotoxic but, instead, appear to act as promoters of the proliferation and establishment of pre-malignant cells. Many of these agents are thought to act by inducing transient non-mutational changes in the expression of certain cellular genes and/or changes in cellular interactions involving membrane structures[44,45]. It has been suggested that electromagnetic fields might act as weak promoters through the induction or potentiation of such transient cellular changes and through this function as co-carcinogens. While some existing studies have sought to explore this possibility the data have yet to reveal a consistent promotional or co-carcinogenic mechanism for electromagnetic field exposure. On this point, however, studies with a mouse cell line transformation system have recently provided somewhat more convincing evidence of a synergistic effect between microwaves and a phorbol ester promoting agent[39].

74   In the light of these continuing uncertainties, it will be necessary to gain a better understanding of the fundamental interactions of electromagnetic radiations with a range of biological systems; specifically, the nature of biophysical interactions at the subcellular, cellular and tissue levels and the possible consequences of these interactions for biochemical, cellular and physiological responses. In the context of this report it is clear that emphasis should be placed on those responses that have a known or suspected association with carcinogenic processes.

REFERENCES

1   Kowalczuk, C I, Sienkiewicz, Z J, and Saunders, R D. Biological effects of exposure to non-ionising electromagnetic fields and radiation: I. Static electric and magnetic fields. Chilton, NRPB-R238 (1991) (London, HMSO).

2   Sienkiewicz, Z J, Saunders, R D, and Kowalczuk, C I. Biological effects of exposure to non-ionising electromagnetic fields and radiation: II. Extremely low frequency electric and magnetic fields. Chilton, NRPB-R239 (1991) (London, HMSO).

3   Saunders, R D, Kowalczuk, C I, and Sienkiewicz, Z J. Biological effects of exposure to non-ionising electromagnetic fields and radiation: III. Radiofrequency and microwave radiation. Chilton, NRPB-R240 (1991) (London, HMSO).

4   Dennis, J A, Muirhead, C R, and Ennis, J R. Human health and exposure to electromagnetic radiation. Chilton, NRPB-R241 (1992) (London, HMSO).

5   Bellossi, A, and Toujas, L. The effect of a static uniform magnetic field on mice. A study of a Lewis tumour graft. *Radiat. Environ. Biophys.,* **20**, 153 (1982).

6   Bellossi, A. The effect of a static non-uniform magnetic field on mice. A study of a Lewis tumour graft. *Radiat. Environ. Biophys.,* **25**, 231 (1986).

7   Bellossi, A. The effect of a static uniform magnetic field on mice. A study of methylcholanthrene carcinogenesis. *Radiat. Environ. Biophys.,* **23**, 107 (1984).

8   Stevens, R G. Electric power use and breast cancer: A hypothesis. *Am. J. Epidemiol.,* **125**, 556 (1987).

9   Regelson, W, and Pierpaoli, W. Melatonin: A rediscovered anti-tumour hormone? Its relation to surface receptors, sex steroid metabolism, immulogic response, and chronobiologic factors in tumour growth and therapy. *Cancer Invest.,* **5**, 379 (1987).

10   Blask, D E, and Hill, S M. Effects of melatonin on cancer: Studies on MCF-7 human breast cancer cells in culture. *J. Neural. Transm.,* **21** (Suppl), 433 (1986).

11   Tamarkin, L, Cohen, M, and Roselle, D. Melatonin inhibition and pinealectomy enhancement of 7,12-dimthylbez(a)anthracene-induced mammary tumours in the rat. *Cancer Res.,* **41**, 4432 (1981).

12   Shah, P N, Mhatre, M C, and Kothari, L S. Effect of melatonin on mammary carcinogenesis in intact and pinealectomized rats in varying photoperiods. *Cancer Res.,* **44**, 3403 (1984).

13   Leung, F C, Rommereim, D N, Stevens, R G, and Anderson, L E. Effects of electric field on rat mammary tumour development induced by 7,12-dimethylbenz(a)anthracene (DMBA). IN Abstracts, 9th Annual Meeting of the Bioelectromagnetics Society, June 1987, Portland, Oregon, p 41 (1987).

14   Leung, F C, Rommereim, D N, Stevens, R G, Wilson, B W, Buschbom, R L, and Anderson, L E. Effects of electric fields on rat mammary tumour development induced by 7,12-dimethylbenz(a)anthracene. IN Abstracts, 10th Annual Meeting of the Bioelectromagnetics Society, June 1988, Stamford, Connecticut, p 2 (1988).

15   Thomson, R A E, Michaelson, S M, and Nguyen, Q A. Influence of 60-hertz magnetic fields on leukemia. *Bioelectromagnetics,* **9**, 149 (1988).

16   Bellossi, A, Desplaces, A, and Morin, R. Effect of low frequency pulsed magnetic fields on tumoral C3H mice — Preliminary results. IN Abstracts, 8th Annual Meeting of the Bioelectromagnetics Society, June 1985, Madison, Wisconsin, p 51 (1986).

17   Byus, C V, Pieper, S E, and Adey, W R. The effects of low-energy 60-Hz environmental electromagnetic fields upon the growth-related enzyme ornithine decarboxylase. *Carcinogenesis*, **8**, 1385 (1987).

18   Cain, C D, Salvador, E Q, and Adey, W R. 60 Hz electric field prolongs ornithine decarboxylase activity response to 12-0-tetradecanoylphobol-13-acetate (TPA) in C3H10T½ fibroblasts. IN Abstracts, 10th Annual Meeting of the Bioelectromagnetics Society, June 1988, Stamford, Connecticut, p 3 (1988).

19   Goodman, R, Bassett, C A, and Henderson, A S. Pulsing electromagnetic fields induce cellular transcription. *Science*, **220**, 1283 (1983).

20   Goodman, R, and Henderson, A S. Sine waves enhance cellular transcription. *Bioelectromagnetics*, **7**, 23 (1986).

21   Goodman, R, Abbott, J, and Henderson, A S. Transcriptional patterns in the X chromosome of *Sciara coprophila* following exposure to magnetic fields. *Bioelectromagnetics*, **8**, 1 (1987).

22   Goodman, R, and Henderson, A S. Exposure of salivary gland cells to low-frequency electromagnetic fields alters polypeptide synthesis. *Proc. Natl Acad. Sci. (USA)*, **85**, 3928 (1988).

23   Goodman, R, Wei, L-H, and Henderson, A S. Induction of the expression of c-myc following exposure of cultured cells to low frequency electromagnetic fields. IN *Transaction of the 7th Annual Meeting of the Bioelectrical Repair and Growth Society*, October 1987, Toronto, Ontario, p 7:85 (1987).

24   Phillips, J L, Winters, W D, and Rutledge, L. *In vitro* exposure to electromagnetic fields: Changes in tumour cell properties. *Int. J. Radiat. Biol.*, **49**, 463 (1986).

25   Phillips, J L, and Winters, W D. Electromagnetic field induced bioeffects in human cells *in vitro*. IN *Interaction of Biological Systems with Static and ELF Electric and Magnetic Fields* (Anderson, L F, Kelman, B J, and Wiegel, R J, eds). 23rd Hanford Life Sciences Symposium, Richland, Washington, October 1984. Richland, Pacific Northwest Laboratory, p 279 (1987).

26   Phillips, J L, Rutledge, L, and Winters, W. Transferrin binding to two human colon carcinoma cell lines: Characterisation and effect of 60-Hz electromagnetic fields. *Cancer Res.*, **46**, 239 (1986).

27   Cohen, M M. The effects of low-level electromagnetic fields on cloning of two human cancer cell lines (Colo 205 and Colo 320). Contractors' Final Report to New York State Power Lines Project. New York, Wadsworth Center for Laboratories and Research (1987).

28   Prausnitz, S, and Susskind, C. Effects of chronic microwave irradiation on mice. *IRE Trans. Biomed. Electron.*, **9**, 104 (1962).

29   Spalding, J F, Freyman, R W, and Holland, L M. Effects of 800 MHz electromagnetic radiation on body weight, activity, haematopoiesis and life span in mice. *Health Phys.*, **20**, 421 (1971).

30   Skidmore, W D, and Baum, S J. Biological effects in rodents exposed to 10^8 pulses of electromagnetic radiation. *Health Phys.*, **26**, 391 (1974).

31   Baum, S J, Ekstrom, M E, Skidmore, W D, Wyant, D E, and Atkinson, J L. Biological measurements in rodents exposed continuously throughout their adult life to pulsed electromagnetic radiation. *Health Phys.*, **30**, 161 (1976).

32   Guy, A W, Chou, C-K, Kunz, L L, Crowley, J, and Krupp, J. Effects of long-term low-level radiofrequency radiation exposure on rats. Volume 9. Summary. Brooks Air Force Base, Texas, USAF School of Aerospace Medicine, USFSAM-TR-85-11 (1985).

33   Kunz, L L, Johnson, R B, Thompson, D, Crowley, J, Chou, C-K, and Guy, A W. Effects of long-term low-level radiofrequency radiation exposure on rats. Volume 8. Evaluation of longevity, cause of death, and histopathological findings. Brooks Air Force Base, Texas, USAF School of Aerospace Medicine. USAFSAM-TR-85-11 (1985).

34   Szmigielski, S, Szudzinski, A, Pietraszek, A, Bielec, M, and Wrembel, J K. Accelerated development of spontaneous and benzopyrene-induced skin cancer in mice exposed to 2450-MHz microwave radiation. *Bioelectromagnetics*, **3**, 179 (1982).

35   Szudinski, A, Pietraszek, A, Janiak, M, Wrembel, J, Kalczek, M, and Szmigielski, S. Acceleration of the development of benzopyrene-induced skin cancer in mice by microwave radiation. *Arch. Dermatol. Res.*, **274**, 303 (1982).

36   Szmigielski, S, Bielec, M, Lipski, S, and Sokolska, G. Immunologic and cancer-related aspects of exposure to low-level microwave and radiofrequency fields. IN *Modern Bioelectricity* (Marino, A A, ed). New York, Marcel Dekker, p 861 (1988).

37   Balcer-Kubiczek, E K, and Harrison, G H. Evidence for microwave carcinogenesis *in vitro*. *Carcinogenesis*, **6**, 859 (1985).

38   Balcer-Kubiczek, E K, and Harrison, G H. Induction of neoplastic transformation in C3H/10T½ cells by 2.45-GHz microwaves and phorbol ester. *Radiat. Res.*, **17**, 531 (1989).

39   Balcer-Kubiczek, E K, and Harrison, G H. Neoplastic transformation of C3H/10T½ cells following exposure to 120-Hz modulated 2.45-GHz microwaves and phorbol ester. *Radiat. Res.*, **126**, 65 (1991).

40   Byus, C V, Lundak, R L, Fletcher, R M, and Adey, W R. Alterations in protein kinase activity following exposure of cultered human lymphocytes to modulated microwave fields. *Bioelectromagnetics*, **5**, 341 (1984).

41   Byus, C V, Kartun, K, Pieper, S, and Adey, W R. Increased ornithine decarbooxylase activity in cultured cells exposed to low energy modulated microwave fields and phorbol ester tumour promoters. *Cancer Res.*, **48**, 4222 (1988).

42   Bishop, J M. The molecular genetics of cancer. *Science*, **235**, 305 (1987).

43   Sagar, R. Tumour suppressor genes: The puzzle and the promise. *Science*, **246**, 1406 (1989).

44   Kikkawa, U, Takai, Y, Tanaka, Y, Miyake, R, and Nishizuka, Y. Protein kinase C as a possible receptor protein of tumour promoting phorbol esters. *J. Biol. Chem.*, **258**, 11442 (1983).

45   Trosko, J E, Chang, C C, Madhukar, B V, and Klaunig, J E. Chemical, oncogene and growth factor inhibition of gap junction intercellular communication: An integrative hypothesis of carcinogensis. *Pathobiology*, **58**, 265 (1990).

4 Residential Exposure and Cancer in Children and Adults

INTRODUCTION

1   Wertheimer and Leeper[1] were the first to claim that electromagnetic (EM) fields from electrical power lines and other domestic electrical wiring might cause childhood cancer. Later they extended their research to adults, and reported[2] that the risk of all cancers was increased in adults who resided near high tension electrical wires. Both studies were conducted in Colorado. The researchers assessed exposure to electromagnetic fields by visiting each address, drawing a map of the electrical wiring and/or transformers in the vicinity and using that information to classify the 'wiring configuration' of each residence into levels of exposure, ranging from low to high. Measurements of magnetic fields near some of the houses were made to validate their classification system.

2   In the last 10 years several studies were set up specifically to investigate Wertheimer and Leeper's hypothesis. The evidence is summarised here, separately for childhood and adult cancers, and for leukaemia and brain tumours, as well as for all cancers combined. As discussed below, the definition and classification of electromagnetic field exposure and of place of residence are often complex and are not always comparable across the studies.

3   It should be borne in mind that epidemiological studies can generate misleading results for a number of reasons, including bias, confounding and chance. In any single study there is scope for identifying an association that may have occurred purely by chance, especially in a subgroup. To minimise this problem the published data are summarised by calculating pooled risk estimates. Where possible, similar definitions and categories of exposure have been used for each study. Wertheimer and Leeper's data are not included in the pooled risk estimates, since they generated the hypotheses examined by others.

4   Combining data from a number of studies can reduce the influence of random variation, but cannot remove systematic errors due to bias or confounding. For example, shortcomings in the method of control selection may lead to similar biases across different studies. Combining the results of such studies clearly cannot remove the bias. In several of the studies reported later, the method of control selection led to controls having a more stable residential history than cases. If, in the areas in which the studies were undertaken, stability of residence relates to the level of EM field exposure (eg through type of neighbourhood or type of dwelling) then lack of comparability will have been created between cases and controls for the exposure of interest. In a similar way, if EM field exposure, or a surrogate measure of it, is associated in several study populations with real but unknown risk factors for childhood cancer (eg population mixing for childhood leukaemia) then a confounder-induced increase in risk will be observed for EM field exposure. It is futile to attempt to minimise or eliminate bias or confounding by pooling across studies in which such effects operate.

DEFINITIONS

Electromagnetic field exposure

Measured magnetic fields

5   Measurements give the most direct assessment of domestic EM field exposure. Field strengths are not constant at all times as they depend on the amount of electricity being used when the measurement is being made (Chapter 2). Some researchers have reported the results of 'spot' measurements made under various conditions of electrical use: often under 'normal' conditions or at times of 'high use'. Others have reported measurements averaged over a 24 hour period.

6   Where possible, measurements averaged over a 24 hour period have been used in this summary. When spot measurements were made at more than one time, those selected have been under normal conditions of electricity use. These measurements are probably more indicative of usual exposure than those made at times of 'high use' of electricity. Where possible, levels of exposure corresponding to 0—0.099, 0.1—0.199, 0.2—0.299 and 0.30+ microtesla (μT) have been used.

Distance from sources of electromagnetic radiation

7   Overhead power lines and electrical transmission stations are a source of high EM field exposure. The distance of a residence from a source of electromagnetic radiation gives some indication of EM field exposure, but it is less reliable than a direct measurement in the home, since the domestic field strength will depend on the nature of the source and on the characteristics of the local electricity distribution. In many studies the source was a high tension overhead line or a substation. The structures that were taken as a source for each particular study are indicated in the summary tables.

8   The distance of a residence from the source of EM field exposure was not always classified in the same way from one study to another. A commonly used division was at 50 m and this value has been adopted here wherever possible, ie whether the residence was closer than 50 m to a source. This is probably a reasonable division for analysis of these studies since exposure to EM fields from sources at distances less than 50 m is likely to outweigh domestic exposures while exposures at much greater distances may not.

Wire configurations

9   This is the least clearly defined way of assessing exposure. The definitions tend to be complex and, although there was some similarity in the classification system from one study to another, few studies used identical systems. For this summary, each research group's own definition of 'high' and 'low' has been used, recognising that these are not comparable across the studies.

Place of residence

10   Most people live at more than one address during their lives. If EM fields are indeed carcinogenic, the time between exposure and onset of cancer is unknown and it is not at all clear which home or address would be the most appropriate for assessing EM field exposure.

11   Most studies have assessed exposure to EM fields at the place of residence at the time of diagnosis of cancer, whereas others have used the place of birth, or even both places. One study selected the house where a child lived for the longest period before his or her cancer was diagnosed.

12   Since most studies report measurements or assessments of EM field exposure at the place of residence *at the time when cancer was diagnosed* for the cases and at a comparable time for the controls, that definition has been used for the summary tables (although it is recognised that this may not be the most appropriate). In some studies data were not given separately for place of residence at the time of cancer diagnosis and these are indicated in the tables.

Cancer sites

13   Where possible, results are presented separately for (a) all cancers combined, (b) leukaemia and (c) brain tumours, as these are the main categories of cancer that have been linked to EM field exposure. Where possible, results are also presented for all cancers except leukaemia and brain tumours.

SUMMARY OF THE RESULTS OF PUBLISHED STUDIES

Childhood cancers

14   All the studies of childhood cancer and residential exposure to electromagnetic fields are of case-control design. Various aspects of the design of each study are summarised in Table 4.1 and these will be discussed in detail later for certain of the key studies.

Childhood cancers and measured electromagnetic fields

15   Direct measurements of electromagnetic fields were reported in three studies: Tomenius[3] and Savitz *et al*[4] studied all childhood cancers, whereas London *et al*[5] studied childhood leukaemia alone.

16   Data on all cancers combined were published by Tomenius and Savitz *et al* using similar, although not identical, categories of exposure (Table 4.2(a)). The pooled test for trend is statistically significant ($p < 0.01$). Tomenius reports results on houses occupied by cases and controls, with more than one household included for a substantial number of subjects. In the computations houses were treated as if they were independent. This assumption will lead to slightly exaggerated assessments of statistical significance, but the effect is likely to be small.

17   For leukaemia and brain tumours the data published by Tomenius and Savitz *et al* are not divided into as many categories of exposure as are the results for all cancers combined. Their results, together with those of London *et al*, are shown in Table 4.2(b) for leukaemia. Overall the highest levels of residential EM field exposure are not associated with a significantly increased risk of leukaemia (pooled odds ratio (OR) = 1.16, 95% confidence interval (CI) 0.65–2.08; Table 4.2(b)) or brain tumours (pooled OR = 1.85, 95% CI 0.91–3.77); Table 4.2(c)), although both odds ratios are greater than 1.0.

18   Leukaemia accounts for 21% of the cancers in the Tomenius study and 28% of the cancers in the Savitz *et al* study. Brain tumours account for 26% and 19% of the cancers in each study, respectively. Table 4.2(d) gives results for all cancers other than leukaemia or brain tumours. The association with high levels of residential EM fields

is strong and highly statistically significant (pooled OR = 2.96, 95% CI 1.30−6.72). Twenty-three children contribute to this finding: seventeen were from the Tomenius study where two of the malignancies were lymphoma, four children had benign tumours and the origin of the remaining eleven cancers is not stated. Six children from the Savitz study contributed to the finding on cancers other than leukaemia and brain tumours; two had a lymphoma, three had a soft tissue sarcoma and for one child the origin of the cancer was not stated.

Childhood cancers and distance to sources of electromagnetic fields

19   Distance from electromagnetic sources such as overhead power lines and electric substations was reported in studies by Tomenius[3], Lin and Lu[6], Coleman et al[7] and Myers et al[8]. The pooled results indicate little association between living within 50 m of a source and all childhood cancers combined (pooled OR = 1.11, 95% CI 0.71−1.73; Table 4.3(a)) or leukaemia (pooled OR = 1.31, 95% CI 0.78−2.21; Table 4.3(b)). For brain tumours, Tomenius reported an excess within 50 m of a source, which was of borderline significance (OR = 3.96, 95% CI 1.00−15.0; Table 4.3(c)), and Lin and Lu reported an odds ratio of 1.09 (95% CI 0.50−2.37) but did not give the numbers on which it was based. It was therefore not possible to calculate a pooled odds ratio for brain tumours. The only data for cancers other than leukaemia and brain tumours come from the Tomenius study (OR = 0.99, 95% CI 0.55−1.78; Table 4.3(c)).

Childhood cancers and wire configurations

20   Assessments of exposure to electromagnetic fields by classification of domestic and nearby wire configurations were made by Fulton et al[9], Savitz et al[4] and London et al[5]. In each study an attempt was made to replicate the original definitions used by Wertheimer and Leeper[1] and this was achieved by London et al. The pooled results indicate a significant excess of leukaemia associated with 'high' compared to 'low' exposures (pooled OR = 1.38, 95% CI 1.08−1.78; Table 4.4(b)).

21   Only Savitz et al present data for all cancers combined and for brain tumours (Table 4.4(a) and (c)) and it is possible to use those data to draw up tabulations for all cancers except leukaemia and brain tumours as well (Table 4.4(d)). A significant excess risk was found for 'high' compared to 'low' exposure wire configurations for all cancers (OR = 1.53, 95% CI 1.04−2.25) and for brain tumours (OR = 2.04, 95% CI 1.11−3.76) but not for cancers other than leukaemia and brain tumours (OR = 1.37, 95% CI 0.84−2.23).

Adult cancers

22   The main published information on electromagnetic field exposure and adult cancer relates to leukaemia.

23   Only one study, by Severson et al[10], included direct measurements of EM field exposure. In that study there was no association between non-lymphocytic leukaemia risk and high levels of EM field exposure (OR = 1.12, 95% CI 0.57−2.18; Table 4.5).

24   When exposure is assessed by distance from electromagnetic sources the combined evidence from three studies (McDowall[11], Coleman et al[7] and Youngson et al[12]) suggests no increase in risk of leukaemia (pooled OR = 1.13, 95% CI 0.94−1.36; Table 4.6(a)). A cohort study of 8000 people living within 50 m of a substation or 30 m of an overhead high tension wire found no excess mortality from all cancers *(Continues on page 73)*

TABLE 4.1 Case-control studies of childhood cancer and exposure to electromagnetic fields

(a) Definition and data on cases

Cases	Study			
	Wertheimer and Leeper[1]	Tomenius[3]	Savitz et al[4]	London et al[5]
Number of cases	344	716	356	232
Type of cancer	All	All	All	Leukaemia
Area	Greater Denver	Stockholm county	Denver Metropolitan area	Los Angeles
Vital status	Deaths	All cases	All cases	All cases
Source	Death certificates	Cancer register	Cancer register and hospitals	Cancer register
Age group (years)	0–18	0–18	0–14	0–9
Calendar period	1950–73	1958–73	1976–83	1980–87
Addresses				
birth	Yes	Yes	Yes	Yes
diagnosis	Yes	Yes	Yes	Yes
other	No	No	?	Yes
Address sources				
birth	Birth certificates	Church district parish records	Interview	Interview
diagnosis	Death certificates or city directories		Interview	

TABLE 4.1 (continued)

(a) Definition and data on cases (continued)

Cases	Study			
	Lin and Lu[6]	Coleman et al[7]	Myers et al[8]	Fulton et al[9]
Number of cases	216	771	374	119
Type of cancer	All	Leukaemia	All	Leukaemia
Area	Taipei	London	Yorkshire	Rhode Island
Vital status	Deaths	All cases	All cases	All cases
Source	Hospital	Cancer register	Cancer register	Hospital records
Age group (years)	Childhood	All (0–17)	0–14	0–20
Calendar period	?	1965–80	1970–79	1964–78
Addresses				
birth	?	No	Yes	Yes
diagnosis	?	Yes	Yes	Yes
other	?	No	No	Yes
Address sources				
birth	?	–	Birth certificates	Hospital records
diagnosis	?	Cancer register	Cancer register	Hospital records

59

TABLE 4.1 (continued)

(b) Definition and data on controls

Controls	Study				
	Wertheimer and Leeper[1]	Tomenius[3]	Savitz et al[4]	London et al[5]	
Number	344	716	278	232	
Source	Denver area birth register File 1: birth month and county order File 2: alphabetical and date order	Stockholm birth register	Telephone directories using random digit dialling; randomly replace last two digits of cases' number	65 friends 167 random digit dialling (random replacement of last two digits)	
Selection	Next birth certificate unless sibling	Birth 'just before or after' case	Eligible telephone responders	Friends: eligible telephone responders	
Addresses					
birth	Yes	Yes	Yes	Yes	
diagnosis	Yes	Yes	Yes	Yes	
other	No	No	Yes	Yes	
Address sources					
birth	Birth certificates	Birth certificates (?)	Interview	Interview	
diagnosis	Death certificates or city directories	Cancer register or church district records	Interview		
Controls per case	1	1	1	1	
Matching	County of registration	Age, sex, church district of birth	Age, sex, 'geographic area'	Age, sex, ethnic group (where possible)	
Risk set ascertainment	No	Yes	Yes	?	

TABLE 4.1 (continued)

(b) Definition and data on controls (continued)

Controls	Study			
	Lin and Lu[6]	Coleman et al[7]	Myers et al[8]	Fulton et al[9]
Number	422	1663	588	240
Source	Same hospital as cases diagnosed	(1) Cancer controls from same registry (2) Population controls from electoral roll	Yorkshire Health Region birth register	Rhode Island birth register
Selection	?	At random	Nearest in time to case	Stratified by year: random selection
Addresses				
birth	?	No	Yes	Yes
diagnosis	?	Yes	Yes	No
other	?	No	Yes	No
Address sources				
birth	?	—	Birth certificates (?)	Birth certificates
diagnosis	?	Cancer register or electoral roll	?	—
Controls per case	?	2 and random	1 (1970–74) 2 (1975–79)	2
Matching	Age, sex, date of hospital admission	Sex, age, borough and year of diagnosis	Sex and local authority area	?
Risk set ascertainment	?	Yes	Yes (partially)	No

61

TABLE 4.1 (continued)

(c) Exposure assessment

Exposure	Study			
	Wertheimer and Leeper[1]	Tomenius[3]	Savitz et al[4]	London et al[5]
Method	Visit houses and map local area	Visit houses	Visit houses	Visit houses
Observations	Electrical wires and transformers	Visible electrical structures and field measurements	Electric and magnetic field measurements in homes and wire configuration codes	Electrical wires and transformers and field measurements
Distances	Measured house to wires with rollatape	Measured by pacing distance by foot	—	—
Classification	High current (HCC) versus low current (LCC) configurations	Distance intervals from electrical structures	Intervals of electric and magnetic fields and wire codes	Intervals of magnetic fields (24 hour and spot) and by wire codes
Blindness to case/control	Partially	Yes	Yes	—
'Confounders' considered	Age, urban/suburban, socioeconomic class, family pattern, traffic congestion, sex	Permanent/transient dwelling, sex, age	Maternal age, father's education, income, maternal smoking during pregnancy and traffic density	Indoor pesticides: hair dyes; black and white TV; father's occupational exposure to spray paint; other chemicals

TABLE 4.1 (continued)

(c) Exposure assessment (continued)

Exposure	Study			
	Lin and Lu[6]	Coleman et al[7]	Myers et al[8]	Fulton et al[9]
Method	?	Grid references of houses	Maps	Map area within 50 m of address
Observations	High tension power lines, transformer or substation	Grid references of substations and pylons	Overhead power lines	Electrical power lines
Distance	?	From nearest source	Measured on map from house to line	Measured house to wires by optical range finder
Classification	Distance from electrical structures	Intervals of distance	Distance and magnetic field estimations	Quarters of distance weighted exposure
Blindness to case/control	?	Yes	Yes, mainly	Not mentioned
'Confounders' considered	None	?	House type	Father's or mother's occupation or education

TABLE 4.1 *(continued)*

(d) Comments on design and methodology

Study				
Wertheimer and Leeper[1]	Tomenius[3]	Savitz et al[4]	London et al[5]	
(1) Some death certificate addresses used as substitutes for missing city directory entries	(1) Control 'diagnosis-date' addresses outside the church district of birth were omitted, but not for cases	(1) Control response to random digit dialling was 78.6%	(1) Control responses to random digit dialling: 82% for cases diagnosed in 1986–87; unknown for 1980–84	
(2) Lack of blindness in original electrical wire observations		(2) Interview rates: 70.8% among cases; 79.9% among controls	(2) Interview rates: cases, 70.1%; controls, 90.3% (in 1986–87)	
		(3) Cases diagnosed 1976–83, telephone dialling 1984–85 – is there a biased tendency to move out of area?	(3) Cases diagnosed 1980–87, date of identifying and interviewing controls not stated	
		(4) Field measurements made in only 36% of cases' homes compared with 74.5% of controls' homes	(4) Field measurements made for 49.5% of cases' homes and 56.0% of controls not stated	
			(5) Wire code assessed for 66.2% of cases and 80.5% of controls	

TABLE 4.1 (continued)

(d) Comments on design and methodology (continued)

Study			
Lin and Lu[6]	Coleman et al[7]	Myers et al[8]	Fulton et al[9]
(1) Only Abstract available, so detailed study methods not described	(1) Purpose of second control group not clear – does not apply to younger leukaemia cases (<18 years of age) anyway	(1) Repeat analysis of earlier work* (2) Errors in matching and selection of cases and controls	(1) Complete addresses used for cases, but only birth addresses for controls

*Myers et al. in Proceedings International Conference on Electric and Magnetic Fields in Medicine and Biology, London (1985).

TABLE 4.2 Childhood cancer in relation to measured magnetic fields

(a) All cancers

Magnetic field (μT)	Tomenius[3,a] Cases	Controls	OR	Magnetic field (μT)	Savitz et al[4,b] Cases	Controls	OR
0.0–0.99	902	751	1.00	0.0–0.99	95	162	1.00
0.10–0.19	159	167	0.79	0.10–0.19	20	29	1.18
0.20–0.29	34	37	0.77	0.20–0.29	3	4	1.28
0.30+	34	14	2.02	0.30+	10	12	1.42

Pooled test for trend (1df) $\chi^2 = 7.33$ (p < 0.01)   Pooled OR = 1.82 (1.09–3.04)
Highest level versus other three levels, Mantel-Haenszel $\chi^2 = 5.17$ (p < 0.05)

(b) Leukaemia

Magnetic field (μT)	Tomenius[3,a] Cases	Controls	Magnetic field (μT)	Savitz et al[4,b] Cases	Controls	Magnetic field (μT)	London et al[5,c] Cases	Controls
<0.03	239	202	<0.20	31	191	<0.268	144	133
0.03+	4	10	0.20+	5	16	0.268+	20	11
	OR = 0.34			OR = 1.93			OR = 1.70	

Pooled $\chi^2 = 0.15$ Pooled OR = 1.16 (0.65–2.08)

TABLE 4.2 (continued)

(c) Brain tumours

Magnetic field (μT)	Tomenius[3,a]		Magnetic field (μT)	Savitz et al[4,b]	
	Cases	Controls		Cases	Controls
<0.30	281	250	<0.20	23	191
0.30+	13	3	0.20+	2	16
	OR = 3.86			OR = 1.04	

Pooled χ² = 2.87   Pooled OR = 1.85 (0.91–377)

(d) Cancers other than leukaemia and brain tumours

Magnetic field (μT)	Tomenius[3,a]		Magnetic field (μT)	Savitz et al[4,b]	
	Cases	Controls		Cases	Controls
<0.30	575	503	<0.20	61	191
0.30+	17	9	0.20+	6	16
	OR = 14.87			OR = 1.17	

Pooled χ² = 6.72 (p < 0.01)   Pooled OR = 2.96 (1.30–6.72)

Notes to table

(a) Data of Tomenius (personal communication) relate to dwellings at birth and cancer registration; more dwellings were identified for cases than controls.

(b) Magnetic field measurements under 'low power use conditions'.

(c) Mean of 24 hour magnetic field measurement in child's bedroom in the house where the child resided for the longest time before the diagnosis of cancer.

(d) Cases are 'nervous system tumours' and include benign tumours.

TABLE 4.3 Childhood cancer and electromagnetic field exposure, assessed by distance from sources of electromagnetic fields

(a) All cancers

Distance from EM field source (m)	Tomenius[3,a]		Lin and Lu[6,b]		Myers et al[8,b]	
	Cases	Controls	Cases	Controls	Cases	Controls
<50	43	31	216	422	20	32
50+	1086	938			354	556
	OR = 1.20		OR = 1.30 (0.92–184)		OR = 0.98	

Pooled χ² = 0.21 (excluding Lin and Lu)   Pooled OR = 1.11 (0.71–1.73)

(b) Leukaemia

Distance from EM field source (m)	Tomenius[3,a]		Coleman et al[7,d]		Myers et al[8,b]	
	Cases	Controls	Cases	Controls	Cases	Controls
<50	5	4	14	15	11	15
50+	238	208	70	126	169	262
	OR = 1.09		OR = 1.68		OR = 1.14	

Pooled χ² = 0.94   Pooled OR = 1.35 (0.73–2.48)   Also Lin and Lu OR = 1.31 (0.72–2.21) (no numbers given)

TABLE 4.3 (continued)

(c) Brain tumours

Distance from EM field source (m)	Tomenius [3,a]	
	Cases	Controls
<50	9	2
50+	285	251
	OR = 3.96 (1.00—15) (Fisher's exact test p = 0.05)	

Also Lin and Lu OR = 1.09 (0.50—2.37) (no numbers given)

(d) Cancers other than leukaemia and brain tumours

Distance from EM field source (m)	Tomenius [3,a]	
	Cases	Controls
<50	29	25
50+	563	479
	OR = 0.99 (0.55—1.78)	

Notes to table
(a) Source = 200 kV wires, substations, transformers, electric railroads or subways. Data include dwellings at birth and cancer registration.
(b) Source = high tension power lines (22 kV+), transformers or substations.
(c) Source = overhead power lines.
(d) Source = substation.
(e) 'Non-solid' tumours.

TABLE 4.4 *Childhood cancer and electromagnetic field exposure assessed by 'wire configuration'*

(a) All cancers

Assessed level of EM field exposure	Wertheimer and Leeper[1]		Savitz et al[4]	
	Cases	Controls	Cases	Controls
High	129	74	89	52
Low	199	257	231	207
	OR = 2.25		OR = 1.52 (1.04–2.25)	

χ^2 for trend = 2.56; p = 0.11 (excludes Wertheimer and Leeper)

(b) Leukaemia

Assessed level of EM field exposure	Wertheimer and Leeper[1]		Savitz et al[4]		London et al[5,a]		Fulton et al[9,b]	
	Cases	Controls	Cases	Controls	Cases	Controls	Cases	Controls
High	63	29	27	52	122	92	113	95
Low	92	126	70	207	89	113	112	103
	OR = 2.98		OR = 1.54		OR = 1.68		OR = 1.09	

Pooled χ^2 for trend = 6.69 (excludes Wertheimer and Leeper)   Pooled OR = 1.39 (1.08–1.78)

Notes
(a) Dwellings at which the child resided for the longest time before the cancer was diagnosed.
(b) Dwellings at birth and cancer diagnosis for cases; but dwelling at birth only for controls.

TABLE 4.4 (continued)

(c) Brain tumours

Assessed level of EM field exposure	Wertheimer and Leeper[1]		Savitz et al[4]	
	Cases	Controls	Cases	Controls
High	30	17	20	52
Low	36	49	39	207
	OR = 2.40		OR = 2.04 (1.11–3.76)	

Pooled χ^2 = 5.24 (p < 0.05) (excludes Wertheimer and Leeper) OR = 2.04 (1.11–3.76)

(d) Cancers other than leukaemia and brain tumours

Assessed level of EM field exposure	Wertheimer and Leeper[1]		Savitz et al[4]	
	Cases	Controls	Cases	Controls
High	36	28	42	52
Low	71	482	122	207
	OR = 1.48		OR = 1.37	

Pooled χ^2 = 0.13 (excludes Wertheimer and Leeper) OR = 1.37 (0.84–2.23)

Note to table
Definitions of 'high' and 'low' electromagnetic field exposure are complex and are given in each paper quoted. In general, authors have attempted to base their definitions on Wertheimer and Leeper's work in 1979[1], but a different definition has been used for each study, except by London et al[5].

71

TABLE 4.5
Adult cancer in relation to measured magnetic fields — leukaemia

Magnetic field (μT)	Severson et al [10]	
	Cases*	Controls
< 0.20	110	134
0.20+	23	25
	OR = 1.12 (0.57—2.18)	

*Non-lymphocytic leukaemia only.

Note to table
There are no data for all cancers or for brain tumours.

Table 4.6
Adult cancer and electromagnetic field exposure, assessed by distance from sources of electromagnetic fields

(a) *Leukaemia*

Distance from EM field source	Coleman et al [7,a]		Youngson et al [12,b]	
	Cases	Controls[c]	Cases[d]	Controls[d]
<50	97	180	137	109
50+	674	1252	3007	3035
	OR = 1.00 (0.76—1.31)		OR = 1.27 (0.97—1.66)	
Pooled OR = 1.13 (0.94—1.36)		SMR = 102 (McDowall[11], see below)		

Notes
(a) Source = substation.
(b) Source = overhead power lines.
(c) Solid tumours as controls.
(d) All haematopoietic and lymphatic malignancies as cases; persons discharged from hospitals as controls.

(b) *Results of a cohort study by McDowall[11]*

Cause of death	Standardised mortality ratio	Number of deaths
All causes	89	814
All cancers	99	212
Leukaemia	102	6
Brain cancer	Not given	Not given

Note
Standardised mortality ratios in 7920 people living within 50 m of a substation or 30 m of an overhead high tension wire in East Anglia.

Note to table
There are no data for brain tumours.

combined, leukaemia, other haematological malignancies or from breast cancer (Table 4.6(b)). No data have been published on adult brain tumours and proximity to electromagnetic sources.

25   There is no information, other than that originally published by Wertheimer and Leeper[2], on all adult cancers and their relation to wire configuration (Table 4.7(a)). The only other published findings on wire configurations and cancer are from one study of non-lymphocytic leukaemia by Severson *et al*[10]. Although the odds ratio is greater than 1.0 in those with 'high' compared to 'low' exposure to EM fields, the excess is not statistically significant (OR = 1.47, 95% CI 0.76—2.87; Table 4.7(b)).

DISCUSSION

26   Most studies of childhood or adult cancer and domestic electromagnetic field exposure have assessed exposure at the place of residence at the time the cancer was diagnosed. This is not necessarily the most relevant exposure for cancer induction since it might be expected that the exposure accumulated over a lifetime or the

(a) All cancers

Assessed level of EM field exposure	Wertheimer and Leeper[2]	
	Cases	Controls*
High	438	372
Low	741	807
	OR = 1.28 (1.08—1.53)	

*Controls were people who died from non-cancer causes.

(b) Leukaemia

Assessed level of EM field exposure	Severson *et al*[10]	
	Cases*	Controls
High	29	26
Low	68	90
	OR = 1.47 (1.76—2.87)	

*Cases of non-lymphocytic leukaemia.

TABLE 4.7
Adult cancer and electromagnetic field exposure assessed by 'wire configuration'

Notes to table
Definitions of 'high' and 'low' electromagnetic field exposure are complex, and are given in each paper quoted. In general, authors have attempted to base their definitions on Wertheimer and Leeper's work in 1979[1], but a different definition has been used for each study.

There are no data for brain tumours.

exposure received at a critical period some time before the onset of cancer would be the most important. The way of assessing EM field exposure in the home has differed across the studies, ranging from descriptions of wire configurations to direct measurements of field strengths. Several studies assessed exposure in more than one way.

27   Direct measurement of EM field strength in the home is, in the short term, more accurate than assessments based on wire configurations or distance from external electromagnetic sources such as overhead power lines, since the EM field strength can be influenced substantially by local factors such as the presence of electrical appliances or by the precise details of the wiring within the home. However, a single 'spot' measurement or even measurements averaged over a 24 hour period do not necessarily reflect cumulative exposure, which would be expected to be most relevant for cancer induction. Distance from an electromagnetic source or local wire configurations may be a more valid indicator of prolonged exposure. With no biological model and little information about the variability and determinants of domestic EM field exposure, it is not possible to state which method of assessment, if any, is best for assessing exposures which might be relevant for the induction of cancer. Since direct measurements of EM fields tend to be correlated with distance from electromagnetic sources and wire configurations[2,5] it might be expected that similar results would be obtained regardless of the measure used.

Childhood cancers

28   The pooled results from published studies suggest a trend of increasing risk with increasing measured field strength when all childhood cancers are combined. When separate types of childhood cancer are considered, there was no significant association between measured high EM field exposure and leukaemia (pooled odds ratio = 1.16, 95% CI 0.65–2.08) or brain tumours (pooled OR = 1.85, 95% CI 0.91–3.77). Indeed the association was strongest for childhood cancers other than leukaemia or brain tumours (pooled OR = 2.96, 95% CI 1.30–6.72). Cancers contributing to this excess included lymphomas and soft tissue sarcoma but the types of cancers contributing to this excess were not stated for half of the cases.

29   When EM field exposure was assessed by proximity to a source of intense field strength such as an overhead power line or transformer, only brain tumours showed a significantly increased risk, although evidence was provided by only one study (OR = 3.96, 95% CI 1.00–15.0). When EM field exposure was assessed by wire configurations, however, the pooled results showed a statistically significant increased risk for all cancers (OR = 1.53, 95% CI 1.04–2.25), for leukaemia (OR = 1.39; 95% CI 1.08–1.78) and for brain tumours (OR = 2.04, 95% CI 1.11–3.76) but not for all cancers except leukaemia and brain tumours (OR = 1.37, 95% CI 0.84–2.23).

30   Thus, for childhood cancers, several of the pooled odds ratio are significantly greater than 1.0 and most that are not significantly elevated are also greater than 1.0. The associations with EM fields were generally strongest of all when exposure was assessed by wire configurations and stronger for brain cancers than other types of cancer. Three studies, by Tomenius[3], Savitz *et al*[4] and London *et al*[5], contributed to the key findings. Before discussing the interpretation of the results, the design of these three key studies will be reviewed.

Study by Tomenius [3]

51   The study by Tomenius included 716 people aged 0–18 years with cancer diagnosed from 1953 to 1973 and 716 matched controls from Stockholm county, Sweden. Of the cancers, 660 were malignant and 56 were benign (mostly benign brain tumours); 294 (26%) of all the cancers were malignant or benign brain tumours and 243 (21%) were leukaemia. The affected children were born and resident in Stockholm county at the time the cancer was diagnosed; the controls were matched by date of birth to the cases and all were born in Stockholm county and resident there at the time the 'case' cancer was diagnosed. Of the cases, 400 (66%) lived in the same church district of the county at the time of birth and of cancer registration; the matching 400 controls also lived in the same district at corresponding times. All the remaining 316 cases had moved from one church district to another within Stockholm county, whereas only 139 (43%) of the matching 316 controls had moved to another church district (the remaining 177 controls lived at the same address on both occasions).

52   Electromagnetic fields in the Tomenius study were assessed at the birth address and at the address where the case (and matching control) was resident at the time of diagnosis. The cases had lived in more dwellings (1.64 per child) than the controls (1.41 per child) because of the method of control selection described above. The biases associated with this are difficult to predict, although it is noteworthy that the controls would have been resident at the same address for longer on average than would the cases. There is, therefore, less possibility of a control dwelling being recently built compared to dwellings of cases. If electromagnetic field measurements are related to the age of a dwelling or the length of time that people live in them, then this could bias comparison of cases and controls.

53   Proximity to sources of EM fields was assessed by Tomenius according to whether a source was visible and the distance to it was measured by 'pacing the distance by foot'. Electromagnetic field measurements were made by Tomenius for 96% of the case dwellings and 95% of the control dwellings (missing values were mostly because the dwelling had been demolished). The EM field measurements were therefore virtually complete for cases and controls. The main potential for bias in the measurements is that they were made knowing whether a case or control had lived in the house being evaluated.

54   The results of the Tomenius study refer to houses rather than individuals, with some individuals contributing more than one house to the analysis. Since the characteristics of the houses that each individual contributes may show greater similarity among themselves than with houses contributed by other individuals, the statistical significance of the Tomenius results is probably overstated. The effect should, however, be small.

55   Perhaps the main concern in the Tomenius study is the large number of houses with high EM field measurement where the cancer site is not specified. Among houses that have EM field measurements of 0.30 µT or more (34 cases versus 14 controls, Table 4.2(a)), the breakdown by type of cancer was: leukaemia (4 cases, 10 controls); nervous system tumours (13 cases, 3 controls); lymphoma (2 cases, 1 control) and 'benign' tumours (4 cases, 0 control). This leaves 11 case houses and 0 control houses with other diagnoses. It is not stated which cancers are included in the 'other' category, yet these cases make the largest contribution to the statistical significance of the results.

Study by Savitz et al[4]

36   The study by Savitz *et al* is more complex in design than the Tomenius[3] study. Cases were aged 0–14 years with a cancer registered or diagnosed in hospital in 1976–83.

37   Only 70% of eligible cases were interviewed and only 36% had electromagnetic field measurements. The authors estimated that 63% of eligible controls were interviewed and that 75% of them (ie 48% of those eligible) had EM field measurements.

38   Controls were identified by random digit dialling (by randomly replacing the last two digits of the case telephone number) during the years 1984–85. The EM field was measured in the dwelling where the case/control was resident at the time of diagnosis of cancer. The controls were required to be resident in the same house from the date when the matching case was diagnosed with cancer to the date when the control was interviewed. This could be for as long as 10 years. By contrast, cases could have moved at any time between the date of diagnosis of their cancer and the date when they were interviewed. Thus controls would have lived longer on average than the cases in the houses assessed. If length of residence is related to EM field exposure this would bias comparisons between cases and controls.

TABLE 4.8   *(a) Father's education and measured EM field exposure*

Paternal education and family income in relation to electromagnetic field exposure and childhood cancer (from Salvitz et al[15])

Measured EM field field (μT)	Father's education					
	Less than college graduate			College or further education graduate		
	Controls n*	All cancers n (OR)	Leukaemia n (OR)	Controls n	All cancers n (OR)	Leukaemia n (OR)
0.0–0.065	47	31 (1.00)	5 (1.00)	49	29 (1.00)	7 (1.00)
0.065–0.099	22	14 (0.96)	4 (1.42)	11	9 (1.38)	4 (2.55)
0.100–0.249	27	18 (1.01)	7 (2.03)	27	13 (0.81)	5 (1.30)
0.25+	8	11 (2.08)	3 (2.94)	10	2 (0.33)	1 (0.70)
TOTAL	104	74	20	97	53	17

(b) Fathers' education and cancer risk

Father's education	Leukaemia		All cancers	
	Cases	Controls	Cases	Controls
College graduate	17	97	53	97
Less than college graduate	20	104	74	104
OR (College graduate : less)	0.90		0.70	

39   The method of selecting controls — by random digit dialling — may well lead to underascertainment of controls from the lower socioeconomic groups and there is evidence that such a bias occurred in this study. The reported effect of an increasing risk of leukaemia and all cancers with increasing measured EM field strength is largely confined to the low income/low education group (Table 4.8). Close examination of these data indicates a low risk of leukaemia associated with high educational attainment by the father (Table 4.8(b)) and with high family income (Table 4.8(d)). This deficit is counter to the general body of data on childhood leukaemia, where an excess is seen for higher socioeconomic status. Moreover, other results from the same study, where children with cancer have been reported to be more likely than control children to live near busy roads[13] and to have parents who smoke[14], provide further evidence of a deficit of low income controls, which could well have arisen in the process of control selection. These observations throw doubt on the overall validity of the study.

Study by London et al[5]

40   The recruitment of subjects for this study was in two separate stages. Children aged 0—9 years who were diagnosed with leukaemia in 1980—84 and selected controls were interviewed in the mid-1980s. When the question of the role of electromagnetic field exposure in leukaemia was raised in the late 1980s, the cases and controls were approached again, and EM field exposure was assessed. Additional cases with

(c) Family income and measured EM field exposure

TABLE 4.8 *(continued)*

| Measured EM field (µT) | Family income | | | | | |
| | <$7000 per year | | | $7000+ per year | | |
	Controls n	All cancers n (OR)	Leukaemia n (OR)	Controls n	All cancers n (OR)	Leukaemia n (OR)
0.00—0.065	54	32 (1.00)	7 (1.00)	44	26 (1.00)	5 (1.00)
0.065—0.099	22	14 (1.07)	7 (2.45)	9	9 (1.69)	1 (0.98)
0.100—0.249	26	19 (1.23)	10 (2.97)	27	13 (0.81)	2 (0.65)
0.25+	10	9 (1.51)	2 (1.54)	8	4 (0.85)	2 (2.20)
TOTAL	112	74	26	88	52	10

(d) Family income and cancer risk

| Family income | Leukaemia | | All cancers | |
	Cases	Controls	Cases	Controls
>$7000+ per year	10	88	52	88
<$7000 per year	26	112	74	112
OR (income $7000+ : <$7000) 0.49			0.89	

*n = Number in category.

leukaemia diagnosed between 1985 and 1987, and controls, were recruited at the same time.

41   In total, 331 cases and 257 controls were eligible for inclusion. The main results on magnetic field measurements were available on only 164 cases and 144 controls and for wire codes on only 211 cases and 205 controls, respectively. Thus one-half of the cases were not included in the comparisons of EM field measurements and one-third were not included in comparisons of wire codes.

42   The method of selecting controls differed according to the year of diagnosis of the corresponding case. For cases diagnosed in 1980–84, half the controls were friends of the cases and half were identified by random digit dialling. No data are available on the number of contacts attempted to identify eligible controls, or on control refusal. For cases diagnosed in 1985–87 controls were identified by random digit dialling; contact was made with 82% of the telephone numbers chosen and 90% of the eligible contacts agreed to be interviewed for the study.

43   Electric and magnetic field measurements were made in one residence per subject and an attempt was made to select the residence 'inhabited for the longest part of the etiologic period', if this address was in Southern California. The rules for selecting residences for measurements are complex and are discussed at length by the authors — 12% of cases and 20% of controls did not have a home eligible for measurement. The biases associated with the method of selecting houses, if any, are difficult to assess from the information provided. However, more cases (43%) than controls (34%) had lived in the house assessed for their entire lives and this suggests that stability of residence affected control eligibility and selection.

44   The main results given by London *et al* show five levels of exposure and adjusted odds ratios from different categories of measured 24 hour magnetic fields and of wiring codes. No effect is seen for measured exposure (except a moderate but insignificant excess for exposures above the 90% point). By contrast, a trend of increasing risk with category of wiring configuration is seen, which is reduced in strength and significance when some putative confounding variables are incorporated in the analysis. Two points can be made about the wiring code analysis. Firstly, the effect of adjusting for the confounders is substantial. The reduction in risk for the highest category, for example, from 2.15 to 1.73, is the most that could be achieved by a dichotomous confounder misclassified 20% of the time. Since most of the confounders in question are not likely to be measured with great accuracy, and are probably only surrogate for other variables, these confounding effects should be taken more seriously than suggested by the authors. Secondly, much of the effect seen for the adjusted relative risk comes from comparing two of the four categories: the 'OL (ordinary low)' and 'OH (ordinary high)', with an odds ratio of 1.87 between these two levels. The overall χ^2 for trend is about 6.0, and the comparison of the 'OL' and 'OH' categories contributes a χ^2 of about 5.5 (approximate calculation using available figures). According to data in table 4 of London *et al*, 'OL' and 'OH' wiring codes are virtually indistinguishable in terms of measured EM field exposures. It would thus seem doubtful whether the trends seen for the wiring codes are really due to the magnetic fields themselves. They may reflect other aspects of housing associated with the different wiring codes. Such an interpretation fits well with the lack of association seen with the measurements themselves.

Childhood cancers: in summary

45   In general, wire configurations have shown a stronger relationship to childhood cancer than other measures of electromagnetic field exposure. One interpretation of these findings is that wiring codes provide a better, even if less direct, long-term assessment of exposure, than measured fields or distance from source. An alternative explanation is that wiring codes are associated with other characteristics of a house, in addition to the EM field exposure, and that the associations of wire configurations with cancer may be due to confounding. This possibility is given credence by the fact that the studies which contribute most weight to the significant results selected controls by methods which may well be biased with respect to socioeconomic status and stability of residence. Furthermore, the proportion of houses for which measurements were made was low.

46   The pooled results also show an association between measured EM fields and all childhood cancers combined, but this result is heavily weighted by a large excess of cancers other than leukaemia and brain tumours (the types of cancer were not stated for half of these) from one study.

47   The weakest evidence of an association between EM fields and childhood cancers is found when distance from a power line or other source is used to assess exposure. Only brain tumour risk was significantly elevated in children living within 50 m of a source. This evidence was derived from one study, where the distance to the source was measured by the researcher 'pacing the distance by foot'.

48   Thus, although the pooled results suggest an association between various measures of EM field exposure and childhood cancer, the contributing studies have sufficient methodological problems to necessitate extreme caution in the interpretation of their findings.

Adult cancers

49   The data on adult cancers and electromagnetic field exposure are sparse, and available evidence does not suggest that EM field exposure is a risk factor.

CONCLUSIONS

50   While there is suggestive evidence of an association between childhood cancer and residential electromagnetic field exposure, the methodological shortcomings of the studies are such that the evidence is insufficient to allow conclusions to be drawn.

51   Information on adult cancers does not suggest that residential electromagnetic field exposure is a risk factor, but data are too sparse to permit firm conclusions.

REFERENCES

1   Wertheimer, N, and Leeper, E. Electrical wiring configurations and childhood cancer. *Am. J. Epidemiol.,* **109**, 273 (1979).

2   Wertheimer, N, and Leeper, E D. Adult cancer related to electrical wires near the home. *Int. J. Epidemiol.,* **11**, 345 (1982).

3   Tomenius, L. 50-Hz electromagnetic environment and the incidence of childhood tumours in Stockholm County. *Bioelectromagnetics,* **7**, 191 (1986).

4   Savitz, D A, Wachtel, H, Barnes, F A, John, E M, and Tvrdick, J G. Case-control study of childhood cancer and exposure to 60-Hz magnetic fields. *Am. J. Epidemiol.,* **128**, 21 (1988).

5   London, S J, Thomas, D C, Bowman, J D, Sobel, E, Cheng, T-C, and Peters, J M. Exposure to residential electric and magnetic fields and risk of childhood leukaemia. *Am. J. Epidemiol.*, **134**, 923 (1991).

6   Lin, S R, and Lu, P Y. An epidemiologic study of childhood cancer in relation to residential exposure to electromagnetic fields. Abstract from DOE/EPRI 'Contractors' meeting, Portland, Oregon (1989).

7   Coleman, M P, Bell, C M J, Taylor, H-L, and Primic-Zakelj, M. Leukaemia and residence near electricity transmission equipment: A case-control study. *Br. J. Cancer*, **60**, 793 (1989).

8   Myers, A, Clayden, A D, Cartwright, R A, and Cartwright, S C. Childhood cancer and overhead powerlines: A case-control study. *Br. J. Cancer*, **62**, 1008 (1990).

9   Fulton, J P, Cobb, S, Preble, L, Leone, L, and Forman, E. Electrical wiring configurations and childhood leukaemia in Rhode Island. *Am. J. Epidemiol.*, **111**, 292 (1980).

10 Severson, R K, Stevens, R G, Kaune, W T, Thomas, D B, Heuser, L, Davis, S, and Sever, L E. Acute nonlymphocytic leukaemia and residential exposure to power frequency magnetic fields. *Am. J. Epidemiol.*, **128**, 10 (1988).

11 McDowall, M E. Mortality of persons resident in the vicinity of electricity transmission facilities. *Br. J. Cancer*, **53**, 271 (1986).

12 Youngson, J H A M, Clayden, A D, Myers, A, and Cartwright, R A. A case/control study of adult haematological malignancies in realtion to overhead powerlines. *Br. J. Cancer*, **63**, 977 (1991).

13 Savitz, D A, and Feingold, L. Association of childhood cancer with residential traffic density. *Scan. J. Work Environ. Health*, **15**, 360 (1989).

14 John, E M, Savitz, D A, and Sandler, D P. Prenatal exposure to parents' smoking and childhood cancer. *Am. J. Epidemiol.*, **133**, 123 (1991).

15 Savitz, D A. Case control study of childhood cancer and residential exposure to electric and magnetic fields. New York State Power Lines Project, Supplement to Contractor's Final Report. (1988).

5 Occupational Exposure to Electromagnetic Fields and Cancer

INTRODUCTION

1   In the last 10 years there have been many studies of occupational factors in the aetiology of cancer that have been thought to have some bearing on the possible effects of electromagnetic fields. These have followed initial reports of an excess of deaths attributed to leukaemia in broad groups of electrical workers by Milham[1] in 1982 and of an excess of brain cancer in similar groups of workers by Lin *et al*[2] in 1985. Subsequent studies have mostly reported qualitatively similar findings, although the excesses have generally been smaller, and some investigators have reported no excesses at all. Measurements of the fields to which the workers were exposed have, however, been the exception rather than the rule and exposures have been presumed to be above the national average on theoretical grounds. The presumption that some members of the broad groups of 'electrical and electronic workers' that have been studied have been exposed at times to above-average levels is certainly correct; but there are as yet no quantitative data for the great majority of the occupations within these groups that would justify classifying the majority of the employees as materially exposed for any substantial proportion of their working lives.

2   The available evidence has been reviewed in Chapter 2. This suggests that the highest workplace exposures are likely to have occurred from the operation of induction heaters and the use of arc-welding equipment. Telephone linemen have also been reported to have substantial exposures, but there must be considerable doubt whether this could also apply to any large proportion of men and women employed in such broad categories as electricians, assemblers of electrical and electronic equipment, and telephone fitters. Only small groups of men are employed on induction heating in any one plant and these men have not been studied as a specific group. Welding, however, is a common occupation and large groups of men have been studied for a variety of purposes, most of whom will have used electric arc welders. The experience of welders may, therefore, provide the best indication of whether or not the sort of electromagnetic fields that are encountered in industrial practice should be considered as a potential cause of the types of cancer referred to above.

OCCUPATIONAL HAZARDS OF WELDERS

3   Electric arc welding produces high concentrations of fumes that are mostly metallic oxides, the type (whether iron, aluminium, nickel, or chromium) depending both on the welding process and its application. Some of the fumes produced are mutagenic and there is reason to think that the chromium and nickel fumes, in particular, are likely to be carcinogenic to humans, causing, specifically, risks of cancers of the lung and nose[3,4]. Many studies of the mortality of welders have, in consequence, been carried out and although most of them focused on the risk of lung cancer several have also provided information about the risks of leukaemia and brain cancer[5]. Other groups of welders have been included in large groups of electrical and electronic workers who have been studied specifically to determine the occupational hazards of electromagnetic fields and particularly the hazard of leukaemia.

4   The results obtained from the study of both categories are summarised in Table 5.1. Altogether 187 cases of leukaemia were recorded against an expected number of

TABLE 5.1
Leukaemia in welders

Study	Type of study	Number of cases			
		Leukaemia		Acute leukaemia	
		Observed	Expected	Observed	Expected
Calle and Savitz[6]	Proportional mortality ratio	20	25.3	13	12.5
Gallagher et al[7]	Proportional mortality ratio	8	8.89	—	—
Juutilainen et al[8]	Cohort	5	5.00	—	—
Milham[1,9]	Proportional mortality ratio	19	21.3	6	9.0
Office of Population Censuses and Surveys[10*]	National occupational mortality	19	20.65	9	11.0
Polednak[11*]	Cohort	0	1.56	—	—
Stern et al[12]	Case-control	7	3.1	—	—
Törnqvist et al[13]	Cohort	39	39.0	—	—
Working Group[14*]	Cohort	6	9.49	—	—
Wright et al[15]	Proportional incidence rates	6	6.24	4	2.99
SUBTOTAL		129	140.53	32	35.49
Cited by Stern[5]					
Becker et al[16*]	Cohort	0	1.2	—	—
Peterson and Milham[17*]	Proportional mortality ratio	—	—	6	3.3
Puntoni et al[18*]	Cohort	15	13.2	—	—
Sjögren and Carstensen[19*]	Cohort	43	43.62	—	—
SUBTOTAL		58	58.02	6	3.3

*Studies undertaken primarily to assess the risk of lung cancer or of all diseases.

Note
Three studies cited by Stern[5] have been excluded: Silverstein et al [20*] because millwrights were combined with welders (4 deaths against 6.94 expected); Puntoni et al[21*] because data were reported only for lymphomas and leukaemias combined (1 death against 0.38 expected); Beaumont and Weiss[22*] because data were reported only for 'lymphopoietic cancer' (4 deaths against 11.4 expected).

198.55 (relative risk 0.94), the results being very similar irrespective of whether the welders were studied primarily to see if they experienced any excess of lung cancer (or any disease in the study by the Office of Population Censuses and Surveys[10]) or whether they were studied primarily as part of a larger group of electrical and electronic workers. In a few instances data were given separately for acute leukaemia. These are also shown in Table 5.1 and lead to a closely similar estimate of relative risk (38 cases against 38.79 expected, relative risk 0.98).

5   Only eight studies have reported data for brain cancer in welders and these are summarised similarly in Table 5.2. The relative risk derived from the pooled series is greater than unity (1.23) and, if it is considered justifiable to compare the total numbers observed and expected, may be considered statistically significant ($p < 0.05$).

OCCUPATIONAL HAZARDS OF OTHER POSSIBLY EXPOSED WORKERS

6   The results of the many other studies of the incidence of mortality from leukaemia and brain cancer in groups or selected subgroups of 'electrical and electronic workers' that have been reported since the initial reports of Milham[1] and Lin et al[2] are examined below under four headings, according to the method of investigation.

Cohort studies

7   The results of 12 cohort studies relating to leukaemia, brain cancer, and, in the few for which the data are given, all other cancers are summarised in Table 5.3. Two studies give only qualitative results for leukaemia, one stating that the relative risk for leukaemia was not significantly 'different from 1.0' and the other implying that the observed numbers of cases from both leukaemia and brain cancer may have been less than expected (Table 5.3, notes g(iii), g(iv) and h(v)). In the combined results of the

Study	Type of study	Number of cases Observed	Number of cases Expected
Englund et al[23]	Cohort	50	37.0
Gallagher et al[7]	Proportional mortality ratio	11	11.34
Juutilainen et al[8]	Cohort	8	9.4
Milham[9]	Proportional mortality ratio	19	18.8
Office of Population Censuses and Surveys[10]*	National occupational mortality	31	21.53
Polednak[11]*	Cohort	3	1.55
Törnqvist et al[13]	Cohort	46	35.4
Working Group[14]*	Cohort	10	9.13
TOTAL		178	144.15

TABLE 5.2
Brain cancer in welders

*Studies undertaken primarily to assess the risk of lung cancer or of all diseases.

TABLE 5.3
Observed and expected numbers of cases or deaths from leukaemia, brain cancer, and all other cancers in cohorts of 'electrical and electronic workers'

Note	Occupation	Leukaemia		Brain cancer		Other cancers	
		Observed	Expected	Observed	Expected	Observed	Expected
a	Professional electrical engineers	2	2.3	2	1.9	20	47.2
b	Power linesmen and power station operators	26	24.6	30	26.2	643	643.4
c(i)	All electrical occupations excluding electricians mainly employed in indoor installations	10 [3	5.4 2.0]*	13	9.9	—	—
c(ii)	Electricians employed in indoor installations. Some categories of iron, metal, woodwork, and chemical process work, printers, etc.	94 [34	77.7 28.4]*	149	128.1	—	—
d	Telephone operations of Telecommunications Administration	12	11.7	—	—	—	—
e	All electrical occupations	16	18.2	—	—	—	—
f	Electricians and electronic workers, welders and metal workers	—	—	121	116.2	—	—
g	Manufacture of telecommunications equipment:						
	men	(iii)	(iii)	5	5.1	—	—
	women	(iv)	(iv)	(iv)	(iv)	—	—
h	Electronic and electrical manufacture	(v)	(v)	(v)	(v)	—	—
i	Amateur radio station and/or operator licence holders:						
	all	36	29.0	29	20.9	676	728.7
	(excluding novices	31	25.4	28	17.9	604	693.0)
j	Electricians	2	1.6	2	1.7	74	81.1
k	Electrical engineers	10	9.9	—	—	—	—
	Electricians	5	6.7	—	—	—	—
l(vi)	All electrically related occupations	334	291.5	250	245.8	—	—

*Data for acute myeloid leukaemia shown in square brackets.

Notes

(a) Olin *et al*[24] — 1254 men entered on qualification 1930–59, followed to end of 1979; mortality compared with that for all Sweden.

(b) Törnqvist *et al*[25] — 10 061 men aged 20–64 years entered as defined in 1960 census in Sweden followed in records of cancer registry 1961–79; cumulative incidence compared with that in all blue-collar workers.

(c) Juutilainen *et al*[8] — all Finnish males aged 25–64 years in defined occupations in census of 1970 followed in files of cancer registry and national mortality records, 1971–80. The expected numbers have been derived from the risk in the 'unexposed' and are, therefore, less than those given by the authors:
(i) probably exposed;
(ii) possibly exposed.

(d)   Wiklund *et al*[26] — all people entered as defined in 1960 census in Sweden followed in records of cancer registry 1961–73: cumulative incidence compared with that in whole population.

(e)   Lindsay *et al*[27] — 10% sample of Canadian workforce followed from 1965 to 1979.

(f)   McLaughlin *et al*[28] — as (d).

(g)   Vågerö *et al*[29] — 2198 people employed for 6 months or more in defined occupations in one of three plants 1956–60, followed 1958–79 and cancer incidence compared with that in Swedish population.
(iii)   15 sites listed for men do not include leukaemia which is classed with residual cancers (12 observed and 28.8 expected);
(iv)   5 sites listed for women do not include either leukaemia or brain cancer which are classed with residual cancers (15 observed and 18.9 expected).

(h)   Vågerö and Olin[30] — all 54 624 men and 68 478 women aged 15–64 years defined in 1960, census, followed 1961–73 and cancer incidence compared with that in Swedish 'general working population':
(v)   relative risk "not significantly different from 1.0".

(i)   Milham[31,32] — all 67 829 men licensed as defined in states of Washington and California between 1 January 1979 and 16 June 1984 and followed in the two state mortality registers until the end of 1984; mortality compared with that in the whole USA.

(j)   Guberan *et al*[33] — 1948 male electricians as defined at the 1970 census and resident in Geneva, studied for comparison with a group of painters and followed 1971–84. Disability rates compared with rates expected from the experience of the Canton of Geneva.

(k)   Blair *et al*[34] — male members of cohort of 293 958 American veterans initially studied to determine effects of smoking. Occupations defined in response to questionnaires in 1954 and 1957, followed 1954–70. Mortality from selected causes among men in each of some 100 occupations compared with that in whole cohort, separately for non-smokers and ever smokers.

(l)   Törnqvist *et al*[13] — 133 687 men aged 20–64 years working in an electrically related occupation according to the 1960 census in Sweden, followed 1961–79. Cumulative incidence compared with that in all Swedish working men born between 1896 and 1940:
(vi)   includes men studied in (b) (d) and (h) above.

other studies[*], leukaemia incidence or mortality was increased by 15% and brain cancer incidence or mortality was increased by 8%.

8   The excess deaths from both diseases among amateur radio station or operator licence holders reported by Milham[31,32] may underestimate the true excesses by a substantial margin. Not only were deaths recorded for a very few years after renewal of a licence, so that sick individuals are likely to be under-represented, but also out-of-state deaths were excluded and comparisons were made with mortality in the whole of the USA, which was generally higher than in the two states in which the subjects lived. After excluding novices, who presumably had practised their hobby for relatively short periods, the relative risk of brain cancer, but not of leukaemia, was greater.

9   Two other studies, which have been referred to in some reviews, are omitted. One is very small[35], concerns only 157 men, and reports only the total cancer mortality (11 deaths against 14 expected). It has the distinction of being one of the very few studies to report measured fields; but the fields, which ranged from about 4 to 29 mT, were static. The other study that has been omitted concerned the incidence of leukaemia in active personnel in the American Navy[36]. Incidence rates were calculated for 95 occupations within the Navy, and the highest but one — and the only one to approach statistical significance — was for electrician's mates. This finding is, however, uninterpretable, as detailed data are given only for the occupations in which more than 3 cases of leukaemia occurred. Mention is made in an appendix to the article of one

---

[*]Excluding data in studies (b), (d), (g) and (h), largely if not wholly included in study (l) of Table 5.3.

other occupation involving potential exposure in which 1 or 2 cases occurred (aviation electrician's mate, relative risk 0.5) but no information at all is given about 57 occupations in which no case occurred and which might, for all the paper reveals, have included occupations with as great or greater potential exposure as the electrician's mates.

Case-control studies

10   Other investigators have studied men with leukaemia or brain cancer and have sought to compare the frequency with which they have been employed in suspect occupations with the frequency reported by other control subjects with or without some other disease. The results of ten substantial studies of this sort are summarised in Table 5.4. Six of these used men who died of other diseases as controls and one[37] used men who were registered as having some other form of cancer. All these used the written record on the death certificate or the registration form as the source of information about the men's occupation. The eighth[12] used as controls other individuals from the same naval cohort matched appropriately with the men who had developed leukaemia, and used the records of the American Navy to define the nature of the men's occupations. All the occupations in these studies may, therefore, be regarded as having been objectively recorded independently of the study. The last two studies obtained information by personal interview and selected matched controls from the same neighbourhoods[42] or from drivers' licence records[44].

11   Three of the four studies which reported data for leukaemia found that the odds ratios for the defined electrical workers were statistically significant. One of these was limited to men dying of acute myeloid leukaemia[39]. The other two gave data separately for myeloid leukaemia and in these the odds ratios were reduced and no longer significant[12,37].

12   In one study[12] some of the men had been exposed to ionising radiation, which was the reason the study was carried out. The doses of radiation were, however, small — mostly less than 1 rem (10 mSv) — and the relationship between leukaemia and employment as an electrician was still present (and statistically significant) when exposures to both ionising radiation and solvents (which were also related to the development of the disease) were taken into account.

13   Another case-control study[46] in which the occupational histories of men dying from leukaemia were compared with those of men dying from other causes has been excluded from the table, although it has sometimes been cited as evidence of an association between leukaemia and exposure to EM fields, as it was limited to coal-miners and used 25 or more years of underground work as a surrogate of exposure. It may be, as the authors suggest, that the presence of overhead power distribution lines and step down transformers and converters and the use of electrically operated trolleys inevitably cause underground miners to have "potentially significant exposure". Yet the authors also point out that "published figures on magnetic field exposures in underground coal mines show the present levels [published in 1974] to be low compared with above-ground measurements in residential areas".

14   Four of the eight studies that reported data for cancer of the brain reported odds ratios that were statistically significant. In the one that was the first to raise suspicion

that EM fields might increase the risk of brain cancers in adults[2] the odds ratio was statistically significant only for histologically confirmed gliomas. Other histologically confirmed brain tumours were excluded and the odds ratio was lower and not significantly raised for tumours classified as brain tumours solely on the basis of the death certificate (and which might, therefore, include secondary tumours arising from other organs). In the study reported by Speers *et al*[41], when occupations were classified according to the industrial classification scheme of the American Bureau of the Census, the odds ratio for men "in occupations associated with electricity or EM fields" was raised (2.11) but not significantly so (confidence interval (CI) 0.77−5.81). When the occupations were reclassified according to the methods described by Lin *et al*[2] the odds ratio for definite exposure (see a(i) in Table 5.4) was infinity (6 cases and 0 controls, $p < 0.01$). In the two studies other than that of Lin *et al*, that included both gliomas and some other brain tumours, the odds ratio for gliomas but not for other tumours was raised in one[42] and was less than unity for both types in the other[44]. Variation of risk with duration of occupation was examined in three studies [40,42,44]. The results are described later.

Occupational mortality studies

15   A third method for seeking evidence of an occupational hazard has been to estimate relative morbidity or mortality rates by relating the numbers of deaths in specified occupational groups to the numbers of individuals said to have been members of the group during a census of the population. This method is substantially weaker than the two already considered as the occupations of the populations at risk and of the people who have developed the disease are obtained in different ways. The Registrar General in England and Wales, has, however, routinely used the method to seek for clues to occupational hazards at the time of the decennial censuses and has drawn attention to an elevated standardised mortality ratio (SMR) for leukaemia in electrical and electronic engineers[10]. The findings for leukaemia, brain cancer, and all other cancers are shown in Table 5.5. Data for acute myeloid leukaemia show a similar pattern to those for all leukaemia (SMR of 128 based on 59 deaths).

16   Another study of this type concentrated on railway engine drivers in Switzerland, a group which, the authors suggest, "probably represents the most heavily exposed occupational category with regard to ELF (0−300 Hz) magnetic fields. Since the Swiss railway network was entirely electrified in the early twenties of this century . . .". Deaths from malignancies of the haematopoietic and lymphatic systems in men aged 20 or more years of age were extracted from the Swiss death register for three groups: railway engine drivers in the period 1969−83 and two control groups which had either a comparable physical environment (C_1, metal construction and machine building) or comparable socioeconomic conditions (C_2, 'technical personnel') in the period 1972−83* and mortality rates were calculated by relating the deaths to the corresponding populations estimated from the censuses of 1970 and 1980. The results showed that the engine drivers had age-standardised mortality rates about midway between those for groups C_1 and C_2 up to 70 years of age, with the highest rates in the metal construction and machine building workers[47].

---

*A change in the classification of occupations prevented examination of these groups in 1969−72.

TABLE 5.4
Odds ratios for leukaemia and brain cancer in 'electrical and electronic workers' estimated from case-control studies

Note	Occupation	Leukaemia		Other cancers	
		Odds ratio	(Confidence interval)	Odds ratio	(Confidence interval)
a(i)	Electrical and telephone company servicemen, linesmen, foremen and engineers; railroad and telecommunication engineers; electricians, electrical and electronic engineers in industry	— —		(i) 2.15 (ii) 1.54	(1.10–4.06) (0.68–3.38)
a(ii)	Electricians (other), dispatcher highway patrolmen, engineers in electric, electronic, aerospace, and telecommunications industries; repairmen, television, electronic service, and telecommunications; welders	—		(i) 1.95 (ii) 1.30	(0.94–3.91) (0.69–2.78)
b	Electricians	3.0 [2.33	(1.29–6.98) (0.77–7.06)]*	—	
c	'Electrical work' previously reported to have increased risk	1.62 [1.16	(1.04–2.52) (0.48–2.84)]	1.01	(0.56–1.82)
d	15 occupational codes defined as electrical	1.0 [1.1	(0.8–1.2) (0.7–1.7)]	1.4	(1.1–1.7)
e	All electrical occupations	[2.1	(1.3–3.6)]	—	
f	Ever in electrical or electronics job Other exposure	— —		2.3 1.0	(1.3–4.2) (0.5–1.9)
g	As a(i) As a(ii)	— —		? 2.86	 (0.82–10.32)
h	All electrical occupations	— —		(iii) 1.8 (iv) 0.7	(0.7–4.8) (0.1–5.8)
i	Electrical engineering industry Electrical and electronic workers	— —		0.9 1.3	(0.2–4.3) (0.7–2.5)
j	Electrical occupation ever any ever high EM field usual any usual high EM field	 — — — —		 0.65 0.80 0.83 0.64	 (0.37–1.14) (0.40–1.64) (0.29–2.33) (0.04–2.07)

*Data for myeloid leukaemia (series B and C) and acute myeloid (series D and E) shown in square brackets.

Notes
(a) Lin *et al*[2] — white males resident in Maryland with underlying cause of death on death certificate:
 (i) glioma or astrocytoma (519 cases);
 (ii) cerebral tumour unspecified (432 cases)
compared with same number of randomly selected controls who died from other causes matched on colour, sex, residence, age, and date of death.

(b) Stern *et al*[12] — 53 white males employed at Portsmouth Naval Shipyard (USA) any time from 1 January 1952 to 15 August 1977 who died with leukaemia as underlying or contributory cause of death (confirmed by hospital records) 1952–80, each compared with four controls selected from nearly 25 000 other employees matched on colour, sex, and age, and, as near as possible, year of birth, first hire, and duration of employment.

(c) Pearce *et al*[37] — 199 004 males aged 20 years and over with cancer and occupation recorded in New Zealand cancer registry 1980–84; men with each type of cancer compared with men with all other types and odds ratios adjusted for age: 534 with leukaemia and 431 with brain cancer.

(d) Loomis and Savitz[38] — analysis of occupations of 2173 men aged 20 years and over who died of brain cancer resident in one of 16 states that report occupations on death certificates and 3400 similar men who died of leukaemia compared with similar controls who died of other conditions matched for year of death (10 for each case): odds ratios adjusted for race and decade of age.

(e)   McDowall[39] — 587 deaths from leukaemia in males aged 15 years and over in England and Wales in 1973, and 1074 controls matched within 5 year age groups but otherwise selected at random from all other similar deaths.

(f)   Thomas *et al*[40] — analyses of occupations of 435 white men aged 30 years or more, dying of brain cancer (death certificate diagnosis validated by hospital record) resident in three areas of the USA in a 3 year period compared with occupations of 386 matched controls dying of other diseases unlikely to be confused with brain tumours (response rates to interview 74% and 63%, respectively).

(g)   Speers *et al*[41] — 202 white males resident in East Texas aged 35—79 years with underlying cause of death or death certificate a 'glial type' brain cancer, 1969—78, compared with 238 controls selected as relating to the next death certificate with same characteristics.

(h)   Preston-Martin *et al*[42]
       (iii)   202 male residents in Los Angeles County aged 25—69 years diagnosed with a glioma in 1980—84 and interviewed;
       (ii)   70 similar men diagnosed with a menigioma;
       each group compared with the same number of controls matched by sex, age within 5 years, and neighbourhood. The patients interviewed constituted 58% of those initially eligible.

(i)   Magnani *et al*[43] — 432 men aged 18—54 years resident in three industrial counties of England (Cleveland Humberside, Cheshire and the Wirral) who died from brain cancer 1959—63, 1965—79, compared with 1603 controls matched for sex, age, and year of death (half matched by county of residence, half by local authority of residence) who died of other causes. Occupations determined from death certificates.

(j)   Lewis[44] — 375 men resident in Gulf Coast area of Texas and Louisiana, aged 20—79 years, with histologically or radiologically confirmed primary neurological tumours of the central nervous system, 1980—84, and 450 age, race, and geographically matched controls. Several methods used to assess EM field exposure with varying results. Data given with use of the method of Bowman *et al*[45] as this was based on field measurements.

17   Both studies also reported data for older men, but the results are not cited here, as the validity of comparing occupations as recorded on death certificates and at census counts in retired workers is too uncertain.

Proportional mortality studies

18   A fourth technique that has been used to obtain clues about occupational hazards is to compare the proportions of deaths attributable to different diseases (or the proportions of different cancers recorded in a cancer registry) in different occupations. The proportional mortality ratios (PMRs) or proportional cancer incidence ratios (PCIRs) can, however, be misleading as an increased ratio for one disease may merely reflect a reduced risk of developing other diseases. Relatively little confidence can, therefore, be placed in such ratios that are raised by less than (say) 50%. The method is, however, easy to use and has frequently been used in the past to seek evidence of possible occupational hazards and it was the technique used by Milham[1] when he first raised the suspicion that leukaemia might occur unduly often in men whose employment involved exposure to EM fields.

19   Since this first report, five other similar proportional mortality ratio (PMR) studies have been reported and Milham has extended his observations[9] to include deaths from leukaemia recorded over a longer period (1950—82 compared with 1950—79) and deaths attributed to several other types of cancer as well. The results of these six studies are summarised in Table 5.6. Only Milham's later results are included as they subsume the first, which had given almost identical results based on 136 cases.

20   In his second study Milham[9] divided his potentially exposed group into two: one presumed to have field exposure to other potential occupational hazards, group (b), and one without, group (a). Both showed statistically significant excesses for

TABLE 5.5
Occupational
mortality statistics
for 'electrical and
electronic workers'
in Great Britain,
1979–80 and
1981–83[10]

		Standardised mortality ratio for:					
Occupation		Leukaemia		Brain cancer		Other cancers	
022.02	Sound and vision equipment operators	154	(2)	63	(1)	114	(43)
027	Electrical and electronic engineers	63	(6)	136	(17)	84	(226)
051	Telephonists, radio and telegraph operators	85	(4)	106	(7)	123	(228)
110.3	Electroplaters	111	(1)	0	(0)	154	(52)
120	Foremen, production fitting and wiring	211	(15)	137	(14)	116	(309)
121	Production fitters, electricians, electricity power plant operators, switchboard attendants	160	(69)	115	(65)	127	(1644)
122	Telephone fitters, cable joiners, linemen	99	(16)	109	(23)	101	(470)
123	Radio, TV and electronic maintenance fitters and mechanics	76	(6)	167	(17)	114	(236)
128	Welders	92	(19)	144	(31)	126	(806)
ALL GROUPS		124	(138)	119	(175)	118	(4014)

*Number of deaths shown in parentheses.

leukaemia, the excess being greater for group (a) than for group (b). For both groups combined the excess was more marked for acute leukaemia (PMR 162 based on 67 cases, not shown in the table) but less marked for myeloid leukaemia, which presumably, with the classification used, was mainly chronic myeloid leukaemia. None of the other studies reported significant excesses, nor was the excess significant when the five others were combined (PMR observed 349, expected 323.06, $p > 0.1$). One, however, showed a significant excess for acute myeloid leukaemia[15].

21   PMR data for brain cancer are available from Milham[9] and from Gallagher et al[7] for workers in British Columbia. Both give values of 123, which, if the two series are combined, is statistically significant ($p < 0.05$). There was, however, no excess in Milham's data in the group that he considered to have exposure only to EM fields without other specific exposures.

22   Milham's PMR study[9] of amateur radio operators is omitted, as the data are subsumed in a later cohort study[31,32].

Cancers other than leukaemia and brain cancer

23   Two other types of cancer have been suggested as possibly related to exposure to EM fields — melanoma and cancer of the breast.

24   Attention was drawn to the possibility that melanoma might be so related when Vågerö et al[29] reported that 12 cases had occurred among some 3000 workers in the

Note	Occupation	Proportional mortality ratio for:		
		Leukaemia	Brain cancer	Other cancers
a(i)	Electrical and electronic technicians, radio and telegraph operators, power and telephone linesmen, radio and TV repairmen, power station operators	159 (45)*	89 (19)	—
a(ii)	Electricians, motion picture projectionists, aluminium workers, welders and flame cutters	128 (101)	136 (82)	—
	(i) and (ii)	136 (146) [126 (29)]†	123 (101)	104 (2402)
b	As (a) plus conductors and motormen, urban rail transit and electrical engineeers	129 (35)	—	—
c	Radio and radar mechanics telephone installers and repairmen, linesmen and cable joiners, electrical and electronic fitters, assemblers (electrical equipment), electrical engineers, electrical and electronic engineers (professional), telegraph radio operators	98 (85) [107 (49)]	— —	— —
d	As (c)	117 (113) [110 (49)]	—	—
e	As (b)	103 (81)	—	—
f	As (a)	103 (35)	123 (52)	—
ALL GROUPS		114 (495)	123 (153)	104 (2402)

TABLE 5.6 *Proportional mortality ratios for leukaemia, brain cancer, and all other cancers for 'electrical and electronic workers'*

*Number of deaths or cases shown in parentheses.
†Data for myeloid leukaemia (series A, C and D) or acute myeloid leukaemia (series B) shown in square brackets.

Notes
(a) Milham[9] — all deaths in men aged 20 years and over resident in Washington State, 1950—82.

(b) Wright et al[15] — cancers in white males recorded in Los Angeles County Cancer Surveillance Programme, 1972—79.

(c) McDowall[39] — all deaths in males aged 15—74 years in England and Wales, 1970—72.

(d) Coleman et al[40] — cancers in males aged 15—74 years recorded in South Thames Cancer Registry, 1961—79.

(e) Calle and Savitz[6] — all deaths in white men aged 20 years and over resident in Wisconsin, 1963—78.

(f) Gallagher et al[7,49] — all deaths in British Columbia in men aged 20—64 years, 1950—84.

91

Swedish telecommunications industry against an expected number of 4.6 (relative risk (RR) = 2.6, CI 1.3—4.5). No consistent trend was observed with duration of employment, nor was the risk limited to any one department. The greatest relative risk, however, was noted to be in departments associated with soldering. In the same year, Olin *et al*[24] reported finding 3 cases of melanoma in Swedish electrical engineers against an expected number of 0.9. Then, 3 years later[50], 10 cases were discovered in a cohort of some 10 000 employees of a large telecommunications company in Montreal against an expected number of 5.0. In this case the study was instigated because surgeons in the local melanoma clinic had noted that 7 affected men had worked in the plant and offices of the company. Reference to melanomas has been made in only two other studies: one large study of all workers in the Swedish electronics and electrical manufacturing industry[30] and another of all electrical workers in New Zealand[37]. The former, which may have included all the cases reported by Olin *et al*[24], recorded 59 cases against 45.4 expected (RR = 1.35, CI 1.05—1.76). The latter recorded 24 cases against 34.3 expected (RR = 0.70, CI 0.46—1.08).

TABLE 5.7
Observed and expected number of breast cancers in men exposed to electromagnetic fields

Study	Type of study	Population studied	Number of cases		Odds ratio (95% CI)
			Observed	Expected	
Matanoski *et al*[55,56]	Cohort	Telephone company employees (New York)[*]:			
		central office	2	0.31	
		technicians	0	0.63[†]	
		other linemen	0	0.45[†]	
Tynes and Anderson[57]	Cohort	Workers with potential exposure to ELF fields (Norwegian census data, 1960)	12	5.81	
Puntoni *et al*[21]	Cohort	Shipyard electricians and welders (Genoa)	0	0.03	
Demers *et al*[58]	Case-control	227 cases recorded over 3 years in 10 registries in the USA and 300 community controls: ever employed in job with exposure to EM fields	33	26	1.8 (1.0—3.7)
Rosenbaum *et al*[59]	Case-control	71 cases recorded over 100 years in New York registry and 256 controls from a cancer screening clinic: occupational exposure to EM fields	—	—	0.8 (0.3—2.0)

[*]Time weighted mean occupational exposure approximately 0.27, 0.24, and 0.16 μT, respectively.
[†]Estimated from data in author's reports.

25   Interest in the possibility that breast cancer might be related to EM fields arose when Stevens[51] drew attention to the experimental findings that prolonged exposure to the electrical fields, described in Chapter 3, might inhibit the normal nocturnal secretions of melatonin in rats[52,53]. It had previously been found[54] that melatonin could reduce the incidence of experimentally induced breast cancer in rats and, on this basis, Stevens[51] suggested that extremely low frequency EM fields might increase the risk of breast cancer in humans by reducing the secretion of melatonin.

26   No occupational studies have specifically reported data that would test this hypothesis in women, but it is clear from the large study of workers in the Swedish electronics and electrical manufacturing industry[30], in which more than 1000 cases of cancer in women were recorded, that the risk cannot have been much raised, as breast cancer is not included in the list of cancers that showed a statistically significant increase, while cancer of the cervix is included (RR = 1.22, CI 1.02–1.47). A few observations have, however, surprisingly been reported on breast cancer in men. These are summarised in Table 5.7. Similar results were obtained in the two substantial studies, a cohort study of Norwegian men employed in electrical occupations[57] (SIR 207, 95% CI 107–361), and a case-control study of men recorded as having breast cancer in ten registries in the USA[58] (odds ratio (OR) = 1.8, 95% CI 1.0–3.7). In the latter study the risk was concentrated in men first exposed under 30 years of age and observed for 30 years or more before diagnosis (OR = 3.3, 95% CI 1.5–7.3) but neither study provided any clear evidence of increased risk with increasing duration of exposure. It is difficult, however, to place much reliance upon the results of the American study, as interviews were obtained in 81% of the 297 eligible men with breast cancer not found to be deceased but in a much lower proportion of the controls (only 65% of households sampled by random digit dialling provided a census of residents and 69% of 240 eligible controls were interviewed, as was a similar percentage of the 239 eligible controls derived from medical records, excluding those found to be dead).

DISCUSSION

Leukaemia

27   The occupational studies that have been reviewed provide no evidence of any excess of leukaemia in welders, for whom there is good evidence of regular and substantial exposure to electromagnetic fields.

28   The majority of the studies of other groups of 'electrical and electronic' workers have found some small excess of leukaemia in broad groups or in some subgroups that have been selected for special study. When, however, all the data are combined, as in Table 5.3 which summarises the results of eleven cohort studies and in Table 5.6 which summarises the results of six proportional mortality studies, the overall excess is very small (Table 5.3, omitting data likely to have been double counted, odds ratio = 1.15; Table 5.6 excluding Milham's original data[1], PMR 108).

29   The excess reported in Table 5.5 can carry very little weight as similar excesses were recorded for brain cancer and for all other cancers combined and the method of investigation involved different types of enquiry to obtain the occupations of the living workers and the decedents. The similarity of the excesses in each of the groups

suggests that they are artefacts of the method of investigation. Somewhat stronger evidence of an excess of leukaemia is, however, provided by the results of the case-control studies summarised in Table 5.4.

30   Two studies not previously considered have reported an excess of, respectively, acute myeloid leukaemia in three groups of electrical workers in a case-control study[60] and of chronic lymphocytic leukaemia in electrical line workers in a cohort study[61], but it is impossible to assess what these findings might mean as they have been selected from larger groups of electrical workers specifically because excesses were found to have occurred in them and no data are reported for the other groups in which excesses did not occur. No reference was made to these other groups by Flodin *et al*[60] but Linet *et al*[61] note that "no excess was seen in other occupational groups [other than electrical line workers] potentially exposed to electromagnetic fields".

31   The accounts of these studies provide evidence of publication bias in favour of reporting excesses of leukaemia in selected groups of electrical and electronic workers and of not reporting deficiencies and there is evidence of such bias in several of the papers that have been reviewed. Examples are given in Table 5.3 (notes g(iii) and (iv)) and by Lindsay *et al*[27]. The last is particularly striking. Howe and Lindsay[62] have followed up a 10% sample of the Canadian workforce since 1965 and have recently extended the follow-up to 1979[27]. An excess of leukaemia in power and telephone linemen was reported personally to Coleman and Beral[63] and published by them in 1988 (7 deaths against 2.9 expected). The complete results for all electrical workers were prepared for publication, but not published until released for inclusion in this review. These showed a substantial deficiency of leukaemia in all other electrical workers (9 deaths against 15.7 expected).

32   It is difficult to know how great an allowance to make for the tendency to report, and to get accepted for publication, evidence of positive effects in favour of evidence that fails to show any such effect, but there can be little doubt that both tendencies are real. Examples have been cited above and Easterbrook *et al*[64] have shown that the tendency in clinical research is common. Publication bias is, perhaps, the most likely explanation for the small overall excess mortality from leukaemia that has been found in the present review.

Brain cancer

33   The position with regard to brain cancer is similar to that for leukaemia in that the combined results of the ten cohort studies listed in Table 5.3 and the two proportional mortality studies listed in Table 5.6 show only a very small excess (Table 5.3, omitting data likely to have been double counted, odds ratio = 1.10; Table 5.6, PMR 123). As with leukaemia, somewhat stronger evidence is provided by the case-control studies summarised in Table 5.4, that followed the initial report[2] of excesses in electrical and electronic workers (two of which were significant) against studies that did not. Unlike leukaemia, however, some excess has been recorded in welders (odds ratio = 1.22).

34   In the ordinary course of events the next step would be to test the hypothesis that the excess was occupational in origin by seeing whether it was concentrated on workers who had been employed for long periods and in periods more than (say) 10 years after first employment in the occupation. Few of the studies have been carried out in such a way as to enable estimates to be derived of the trends in risk with either of

these factors, but three case-control studies have provided evidence of a trend with duration of employment. Their results are summarised in Table 5.8. Two show significant increases with duration; one shows a slightly higher risk for usual

Study	Occupation	Subjects	0	<5	5–19	≥20	P for trend
			Number of men with duration of employment (years) of:				
Thomas *et al*[40]	Exposure to MW/RF radiation in an electrical or electronic job	Cases[a]	359	8	11	22	
		Controls	341	8	3	7	<0.05
		Relative risk	1.0	1.1	3.7	3.1	
	Exposure but never in electrical or electronic job	Cases[a]	359	10	7	7	
		Controls	341	9	5	8	>0.05
		Relative risk	1.0	1.0	1.5	1.0	
	Exposure in electronics manufacture and repair	Cases[b]	246	10	6	8	
		Controls	341	4	1	1	<0.05
		Relative risk	1.0	3.3	7.6	10.4	
	Exposure as electrical tradesmen	Cases[b]	246	7	3	6	
		Controls	341	6	4	4	>0.05
		Relative risk	1.0	1.6	1.0	2.6	
Preston-Martin *et al*[42]	Electrical engineers, radio and telegraph operators, electricians and apprentices, data processing machine repairmen, household appliance and accessory installers and mechanics, office machine mechanics and repairmen, radio and television repairmen, telephone linemen and splicers	Cases[b]	172	16	14		
		Controls	182	12	8		0.05
		Relative risk	1.0	1.4	1.8		

Study	Occupation	Odds ratio	95% CI
		Employment of 10 or more years compared with none or less	
Lewis[44]	Electrical and electronic occupations defined by Bowman *et al*[45]		
	ever employed	0.85[c]	(0.32–2.22)
	usually employed	1.08[c]	(0.37–2.97)

Notes
(a) Brain cancers.
(b) Gliomas.
(c) Compared with odds ratios for any duration of employment of 0.05 and 0.83 in Table 5.4.

employment compared with any. Two cohort studies have also provided some information about the trend with time since first exposure. The Working Group study[14] of European welders provides no suggestion of an overall excess mortality from brain cancer (10 deaths against 9.13 expected) but it does show a greater mortality more than 20 years after first employment than earlier (SMR 152, based on 6 deaths, against SMR 77, based on 4 deaths) (Working Group, personal communication). Milham's study[31,32] of amateur radio station and operator licence holders also shows a small increase in risk when novices (who may be presumed to have been actively practising the hobby for a relatively short period) are excluded (SMR 156 against 139, Table 5.3). These two pieces of evidence are quantitatively weak or else dependent for their strength on division of 'electrical workers' into arbitrarily determined subgroups; but they do give some support to the idea that there has been a specific occupational hazard of brain gliomas in association with at least some types of electrical or electronic work.

35   Against this idea, it may be noted, firstly, that the excess in electrical and electronic workers in the British national occupational study[10] was less than the excess of leukaemia (Table 5.5), which, it has been suggested, is an artefact produced by the non-comparability of the numerator and denominator, and, secondly, that a substantial number of studies that could have given data on brain cancer have not done so, thus providing an opportunity for publication bias to have affected the results.

36   On balance the weight of evidence is weakly in favour of the existence of an occupational hazard in association with welding and at least with some other types of electrical and electronic work. If such a hazard does exist it would be compatible with an effect of electromagnetic fields or with an effect from some occupational associated chemical carcinogen. In the absence of evidence of an increase in risk with increasing level of exposure, the conclusion can be only that an occupational hazard of brain cancer from exposure to electromagnetic fields is possible but not proven.

Other cancers

37   The small excesses of melanoma that have been reported seem likely to be the sort of chance findings that must be expected to occur when many studies are undertaken and many types of cancer are examined. The same might be true of the excess of breast cancer in men reported in the Norwegian cohort[57] but could hardly be held to explain the findings in the large case-control study in the USA[58]. This was carried out at a time when the hypothesis that breast cancer might be related to EM fields was not well recognised and the results are unlikely to be due to recall bias. The poor participation rate by those approached to act as potential controls makes it impossible to accept the reported results of EM fields on melatonin secretion at their face value, but the possible effect of melatonin on the risk of cancer leaves open the question of an effect on the incidence of breast cancer in humans.

Assessment of evidence

38   Attribution of the risk of cancer to an occupational hazard can be relatively simple if the occupation involves exposure to an agent that has been shown to cause cancer in animals in doses that are not generally toxic. In the absence of such experimental evidence, the interpretation of human evidence can be exceptionally difficult. It is not difficult if the observed risk is grossly elevated, as was, for example, the risk of nasal

sinus cancer in men employed in the refining of nickel or in the manufacture of hardwood furniture, but such observations are made only rarely and the problem with which scientists are commonly faced is one in which the risk of a particular type of cancer has been observed to be increased by only a small amount, based on numbers that make the excess only moderately significant in statistical terms. In this situation, the conclusion that an excess was attributable to a specific occupational hazard can be reached only after the finding has been confirmed in other studies, bias and confounding with other hazards have been considered and dismissed, and the excess has been shown to have the features that are characteristic of occupational risks: namely, that the risk occurs after an appropriate induction period (which will differ with different types of cancer) and that it is quantitatively related to the dose of the agent to which individuals have been occupationally exposed. The last feature is particularly important, but can seldom be evaluated in precise terms and, in these circumstances, duration of exposure may have to serve as a relatively poor surrogate.

39   In the present situation, the evidence to suggest that exposure to extremely low frequency EM fields presents an occupational hazard is extremely weak. It provides no reason to think that the reported excesses of any type of cancer other than leukaemia, cancer of the brain, and cancer of the breast in men are anything other than the chance findings that must be expected to occur when many types are examined in many studies.

40   The large number of observations relating to leukaemia show, in total, only a very small increase in risk, which has not been shown to have any of the specific features of occupational cancer, and may well be due to bias in favour of publishing results that suggest a hazard rather than the reverse.

41   Whether the same could apply to the reported excess of brain cancer is less clear. The evidence is a little more consistent and there is some to suggest that the excess increases with duration of employment. Confounding cannot be eliminated, as exposure to EM fields has commonly been accompanied by exposure to a variety of chemicals. However, no causes of brain cancer are known other than hereditary anomalies and ionising radiation, and it is therefore impossible either to allow for them or to say that no allowance is necessary. In the absence of evidence that an increased risk of brain cancer occurs after an appropriate induction period and is quantitatively related to some measure of exposure, it can be concluded only that the evidence suggests that occupational exposure to EM fields may cause a hazard of brain cancer, but that it is far from certain that it does.

42   The few reports of breast cancer in men do not allow any conclusion to be drawn, but the experimental evidence is suggestive enough to justify further investigation of the possibility that EM fields may cause an occupational hazard of this normally rare disease.

CONCLUSIONS

43   The many investigations into the possibility of an occupational hazard of cancer from exposure to extremely low frequency electromagnetic fields have not provided any evidence of a quantitative relationship between risk and level of exposure.

44   The very small excess risk of leukaemia in the total data may be attributed to selection bias in favour of the publication of positive results. The greater excess of brain cancer may indicate an occupational hazard from some types of electronic work but the nature of the hazard (if it exists) is unclear. No conclusion can be drawn from the reports of excesses of other types of cancer, but the experimental evidence justifies further investigation of an occupational hazard of breast cancer for men.

REFERENCES

1   Milham, S. Mortality from leukaemia in workers exposed to electrical and magnetic fields. *N. Engl. J. Med.,* **307**, 249 (1982).

2   Lin, R S, Dischinger, P C, Conde, J, and Farrel, K P. Occupational exposure to electromagnetic fields and the occurrence of brain tumours. *J. Occup. Med.,* **27**, 413 (1985).

3   International Agency for Research on Cancer. *Some Metals and Metallic Compounds.* Lyon, IARC Monographs on the Evaluation of the Carcinogenic Risk of Chemicals to Humans, Volume 23 (1980).

4   International Committee on Nickel Carcinogenesis in Man. Report of the International Committee on Nickel Carcinogenesis in Man. *Scand. J. Work Environ. Health,* **16**, 1 (1990).

5   Stern, R M. Cancer incidence among welders: Possible effects of exposure to extremely low frequency electromagnetic radiation (ELF) and to welding fumes. *Environ. Health Perspect.,* **76**, 221 (1987).

6   Calle, E E, and Savitz, D A. (1985). Leukaemia in occupational groups with presumed exposure to electrical and magnetic fields. *N. Engl. J. Med.,* **313**, 1476 (1985).

7   Gallagher, R P, Threlfall, W J, Band, P R, and Spinelli, J J. *Occupational Mortality in British Columbia 1950–1984.* Vancouver, Cancer Control Agency of British Columbia (1989).

8   Juutilainen, J, Läärä, E, and Pukkala, E. Incidence of leukaemia and brain tumours in Finnish workers exposed to ELF magnetic fields. *Arch. Occup. Environ. Health,* **62**, 289 (1990).

9   Milham, S. Mortality in workers exposed to electromagnetic fields. *Environ. Health Perspect.,* **62**, 297 (1985).

10   Office of Population Censuses and Surveys. *Occupational Mortality, Great Britain 1979–80.* London, HMSO (1986).

11   Polednak, A P. Mortality among welders including a group exposed to nickel oxide. *Arch. Environ. Health,* **26**, 235 (1981).

12   Stern, F B, Waxweiler, R A, Beaumont, J J, Lee, S T, Rinsky, R A, Zukmwalde, R D, Halperin, W E, Bierraum, P J, Landrigan, P J, and Murray, W E. A case-control study of leukaemia at a naval nuclear shipyard. *Am. J. Epidemiol.,* **123**, 980 (1986).

13   Törnqvist, S, Knave, B, Ahlbom, A, and Persson, T. Incidence of leukaemia and brain tumours in some "electrical occupations". *Br. J. Ind. Med.,* **48**, 597 (1991).

14   Working Group. A historical perspective study of European stainless steel, mild steel, and shipyard welders. *Br. J. Ind. Med.,* **48**, 148 (1991).

15   Wright, W E, Peters, J M, and Mack, T M. Leukaemia in workers exposed to electrical and magnetic fields. *Lancet,* **2**, 1160 (1982).

16   Becker, N, Claude, J, and Frentzel-Beymer. Cancer risk of arc welders exposed to fumes containing chromium and nickel. *Scand. J. Work Environ. Health,* **4**, 75 (1985).

17   Peterson, G R, and Milham, S. Occupational mortality in the state of California, 1959–61. Washington DC, Department of Health, Education and Welfare, NIOSH, No. 104 (1980).

18   Puntoni, R, Vercelli, M, Ceppi, M, Valerio, F, Di Georgio, F, Gogioso, L, Bonassi, S, Alloro, G, Filiberti, R, and Santi, L. Epidemiological investigation on causes of death among dockyard workers by type and length of exposure (1960–1980). IN *Proceedings International Conference on Risk Assessment of Occupational Exposure in the Harbour Environment,* Genoa, October 1984, pp 43–54 (1984).

19 Sjögren, B, and Carstensen, J. Cancer morbidity among Swedish welders and gas cutters. IN *Health Hazards and Biological Effects of Welding Fumes and Gases* (R M Stern, A Berlin, A C Fletcher, and J Järvisalo eds.) Amsterdam, Elsevier Biomedical Press, Excerpta Medica (1986).

20 Silverstein, M, Maizlish, N, Park, R, and Mirer, F. Mortality among workers exposed to coal tar pitch volatiles and welding emissions: An exercise in epidemiologic triage. *Am. J. Public Health,* **75**, 1283 (1985).

21 Puntoni, R, Vercelli, M, Merlo, F, Valerio, F, and Santi, L. Mortality among shipyard workers in Genoa. *Ann. N.Y. Acad. Sci.,* **330**, 353 (1979).

22 Beaumont, J J, and Weiss, N S. Mortality of welders, ship fitters and other metal trades workers in Boilermakers local no. 104 AFL-C10. *Am. J. Epidemiol.,* **112**, 775 (1980).

23 Englund, A, Ekman, G, and Zabrielski, L. Occupational categories among brain tumour cases recorded in the cancer registry in Sweden. *Ann. N.Y. Acad. Sci.,* **381**, 188 (1982).

24 Olin, R, Vågerö, D, and Ahlbom, A, Morbidity experience of electrical engineers. *Br. J. Ind. Med.,* **42**, 211 (1985).

25 Törnqvist, S, Norell, S, Ahlbom, A, and Knave, B. Cancer in the electric power industry. *Br. J. Ind. Med.,* **43**, 212 (1986).

26 Wiklund, K, Einhorn, J, and Eklund, G. An application of the Swedish cancer environment registry. Leukaemia among telephone operators at the telecommuncations administration in Sweden. *Int. J. Epidemiol.,* **10**, 373 (1981).

27 Lindsay, J P, Green, L M, and Howe, G R. Mortality from leukaemia and non-Hodgkin's lymphoma amongst electrical workers. Unpublished letter, reported personally (1991).

28 McLaughlin, J K, Malker, H S R, Blot, W J, Malker, B K, Stone, B J, Weiner, J A, Ericsson, J L E, and Fraumeni, J. Occupational risks for intracranial gliomas in Sweden. *J. Natl Cancer Inst.,* **78**, 253 (1987).

29 Vågerö, D, Ahlbom, A, Olin, R, and Ahlsten, S. Cancer morbidity among workers in the telecommunications industry. *Br. J. Ind. Med.,* **42**, 191 (1985).

30 Vågerö, D, and Olin, R. Incidence of cancer in the electronics industry: Using the new Swedish Cancer Environment Registry. *Br. J. Ind. Med.,* **40**, 188 (1983).

31 Milham, S. Increased mortality in amateur radio operators due to lymphatic and haematopoietic malignancies. *Am. J. Epidemiol.,* **127**, 50 (1988).

32 Milham, S. Mortality by license class in amateur radio operators. *Am. J. Epidemiol.,* **128**, 1175 (1988).

33 Guberan, E, Usel, M, Raymond, L, Tissot, R, and Sweetnam, P M. Disability, mortality, and incidence of cancer among Geneva painters and electricians: A historical perspective study. *Br. J. Ind. Med.,* **46**, 16 (1989).

34 Blair, A, Walrath, J, and Rogot, E. Mortality patterns among US veterans by occupation. I. Cancer. *J. Natl Cancer Inst.,* **75**, 1039 (1985).

35 Barregård, L, Järvolm, R, and Ungethum, E. Cancer among workers exposed to strong static magnetic fields. *Lancet,* **2**, 892 (1985).

36 Garland, F C, Shaw, E, Gorham, E D, Garland, C F, White, M R, and Sinsheimer, P J. Incidence of leukaemia in occupations with potential electromagnetic field exposure in United States Navy personnel. *Am. J. Epidemiol.,* **132**, 293 (1990).

37 Pearce, N, Reif, J, and Fraser, J. Case-control studies of cancer in New Zealand electrical workers. *Int. J. Epidemiol.,* **18**, 55 (1989).

38 Loomis, D P, and Savitz, D A. Mortality from brain cancer and leukaemia among electrical workers. *Br. J. Ind. Med.,* **47**, 633 (1990).

39 McDowall, M E, Leukaemia mortality in electrical workers in England and Wales. *Lancet,* **1**, 246 (1983).

40 Thomas, T L, Stolley, P D, Stemhagen, A. Fontham, E T H, Bleeker, M L, Stewart, R A, and Hoover, R N. Brain tumour mortality risk among men with electrical and electronic jobs: A case-control study. *J. Natl Cancer Inst.,* **79**, 223 (1987).

41 Speers, M A, Dobbins, J G, and Van Miller, S. Occupational exposure and brain cancer mortality: A preliminary study of East Texas residents. *Am. J. Ind. Med.,* **13**, 629 (1988).

42   Preston-Martin, S, Mack, W, and Henderson, B E. Risk factors for gliomas and meningiomas in males in Los Angeles County. *Cancer Res.,* **49**, 6137 (1989).

43   Magnani, C, Coggon, D, Osmond, C, and Acheson, E D. Occupation and five cancers: A case-control study using death certificates. *Br. J. Ind. Med.,* **44**, 769 (1987).

44   Lewis, R J. A case-control comparison interview study of brain tumours and employment in occupation with presumed electric and magnetic field exposures. Houston, Unversity of Texas School of Public Health, Dissertation for degree of Doctor of Philosophy (1990).

45   Bowman, J D, Garabrant, D H, Sobel, E, *et al.* Exposures to extremely low frequency (ELF) electromagnetic fields in occupations with elevated leukaemia rates. *Appl. Ind. Hyg.,* **3**, 189 (1988).

46   Gilman, P A, Ames, R G, and McCawley, M A. Leukaemia risk among US white male coal miners: A case-control study. *J. Occup. Med.,* **27**, 669 (1985).

47   Balli-Antunes, M, Pfluger, D H, and Minder, C E. The mortality from malignancies of haematopoietic and lymphatic systems (MHLS) among railway engine drivers. *Environmetrics,* **1**, 121 (1990).

48   Coleman, M, Bell, J, and Skeet, R. Leukaemia incidence in electrical workers. *Lancet,* **1**, 982 (1983).

49   Gallagher, R P, McBride, M L, Band, P R, Spanelli, J J, Threlfall, W J, and Yang, P. Occupational electromagnetic field exposure, solvent exposure, and leukaemia. *J. Occup, Med.,* **32**, 64 (1990).

50   De Guire, L, Thériault, G, Iturra, H, Provencher, S, Cyr, D, and Case, B W. Increased incidence of malignant melanoma of the skin in a telecommunications industry. *Br. J. Ind. Med.,* **45**, 824 (1988).

51   Stevens, R G. Electric power use and breast cancer: A hypothesis. *Am. J. Epidemiol.,* **125**, 556 (1987).

52   Wilson, B W, Anderson, L E, and Hilton, D I. Chronic exposure to 60 Hz electric fields: Effects on pineal function in the rat. *Bioelectromagnetics,* **2**, 371 (1981).

53   Wilson, B W, Anderson, L E, and Hilton, D I. Chronic exposure to 60 Hz electric fields: Effects on pineal function in the rat. *Bioelectromagnetics,* **4**, 293 (1983).

54   Tamarkin, L, Cohen, M, and Roselle, D. Melatonin inhibition and pinealectomy enhancement of 7,12-dimethylbenz(a)anthacene-induced mammary tumours in the rat. *Cancer Res.,* **41**, 4432 (1981).

55   Matanoski, G M, Elliott, E A, and Breysse, P N. Cancer incidence in New York telephone workers. Poster presented at the Annual Review of Research on Biological Effects of 50/60 Hz Electric and Magnetic Fields, (organised by the US Department of Energy). Portland, Oregon, November 1989.

56   Matanoski, G M, Breysse, P N, and Elliott, E A. Electromagnetic field exposure and male breast cancer. *Lancet,* **337**, 737 (1991).

57   Tynes, T, and Andersen, A. Electromagnetic fields and male breast cancer. *Lancet,* **336**, 1596 (1990).

58   Demers, P A, Thomas, D B, Sternhagen, A, Thompson, W D, Curnen, M G M, Satariano, W, Austin, D F, Isaacson, P, Greenberg, R S, Key, C, Kolonel, L K, and West, D W. Occupational exposure to electromagnetic fields and breast cancer in men. *Am. J. Epidemiol.,* **134**, 340 (1991).

59   Rosenbaum, P, Vena, J, Zielezny, M, and Michelek, A. Risk factors for male breast cancer in Western New York. Abstract presented at Society for Epidemiologic Research, Snowbird, Utah, June 1990.

60   Flodin, U, Fredriksson, M, Axelson, O, Persson, B, and Hardell, L. Background radiation, electrical work, and some other exposures associated with acute myeloid leukaemia in a case-referent study. *Arch. Environ Health,* **41**, 77 (1986).

61   Linet, M S, Malker, H S R, McLaughlin, J K, Weiner, J A, Stone, B J, Blot, W J, Ericsson, J L E, and Fraumeni, J F. Leukaemias and occupation in Sweden: A registry-based analysis. *Am. J. Ind. Med.,* **14**, 319 (1988).

62   Howe, G R, and Lindsay, J P. A follow-up study of a ten per cent sample of the Canadian Labour Force. I. Cancer mortality in males 1965–73. *J. Natl Cancer Inst.,* **70**, 37 (1983).

63   Coleman, M, and Beral, V. A review of epidemiological studies of the health effects of living near or working with electricity generation and transmission equipment. *Int. J. Epidemiol.,* **17**, (1988).

64   Easterbrook, P J, Berlin, J A, Gopalan, R, and Matthews, D R. Publication bias in clinical research. *Lancet,* **337**, 867 (1991).

6 Paternal Occupational Exposure to Electromagnetic Fields and Childhood Cancer

INTRODUCTION

1   Several studies of the relationships between childhood cancer and the potential for paternal occupational exposure to electromagnetic fields have been reported. None has involved any direct measurements of the fields, and the categorisation of potential exposure has been determined mainly through occupational and industrial descriptions using exposure-linkage techniques.

EPIDEMIOLOGICAL STUDIES

2   The studies reported have all been of the case-control type. The cases have typically been ascertained through the use of death certificates or cancer registrations for children under 15 years of age in a defined geographical area during a certain calendar period. Controls have mainly been identified from the same birth register as that in which the affected children's births were entered with one or more controls being selected for each case. The selection of controls has usually been described as 'at random' from lists of children with the same year of birth as the affected children, matched, in some studies, for sex, race, or county of residence. In only one of the main studies reported has follow-up been carried out to find out whether the controls were resident in the geographical area of case ascertainment at the date of diagnosis of the matched case and hence a member of the at-risk set.

EXPOSURE ASSESSMENT

3   In most studies exposure assessment has been based on the occupation and industry recorded for the father on the birth certificate of the child. This gives information on reported employment at the time of birth only, and does not consider previous jobs and potential for earlier (or subsequent) exposures. The occupational and industrial descriptions on the birth certificates are typically coded according to governmental classification schemes that were not designed for epidemiological purposes, such as the Dictionary of Occupational Titles and the Standard Industrial Classification system. Their mode of usage in the studies discussed here is described in a number of publications[1-4].

4   The next step after this coding is to classify the occupational and industrial codes according to their potential for association with exposure to electromagnetic fields in a few qualitatively defined categories[1-3]. This was done independently of the particular studies of childhood cancer and paternal exposure discussed below. Unfortunately the categories used differed in the different studies and this complicates the assessment of the overall results.

SPECIFIC TYPES OF CANCER
Nervous system tumours

5   Three published case-control studies have specifically reported on nervous system tumours in children in Ohio[5], New York[6], and Texas[7]. The first study included only brain tumours (International Classification of Diseases code 193.0 period in the 7th revision and 191 in the 8th revision), the second study included central nervous system tumours, and the third study included intracranial and spinal cord tumours (for the last two studies the ICD rubrics are not given).

6   The first and third studies used birth certificates to obtain data on paternal occupation and industry with exposure classification methods as outlined above. In the second study telephone interviews with mothers were carried out using a structured questionnaire asking about occupation and industry at the time of birth and of diagnosis, with a response rate of 70% for the controls and 85% for the cases.

7   In the third study, coding of data was said to be carried out without knowledge of the status of the child (case or control); but no mention was made of whether any such 'blindness' was achieved for the other two studies, nor whether it was achieved during the telephone interviews in the second study. In the first study adjustments were made for parental age, birth order, birthweight, sex, year of birth and rural or urban status of mother's county of residence at the time of birth of the child, and in the second study adjustments were made for year of birth, sex and race, but these did not modify the findings. In the third study possible confounding variables were not considered.

8   The published results are summarised in Table 6.1. In each case the odds ratio for paternal exposure was greater than unity, but was statistically significant only in subgroups selected as having the highest odds ratios. Consistent comparisons between studies can be made only between overall categories in the second and third studies, in both of which odds ratios of about 1.5 were found. Only in the second study were paternal occupations at both the time of diagnosis and at the child's birth considered, and in this study the odds ratio for paternal exposure to electromagnetic fields was higher for occupation at the child's birth.

9   Aspects of design of the studies are given in Table 6.2; a summary of the results is presented in Table 6.3.

10   Childhood nervous system tumours have also been included in about six further studies of childhood cancer and paternal occupation according to a recent review[8]. None of these studies indicated any raised odds ratio associated with potential paternal exposure to electromagnetic fields, although they were mainly published before the concern about electromagnetic fields arose and it is not always clear that such relationships were investigated. Two more recent studies add little to the available evidence. The first is a wide-ranging study of paternal occupation where jobs involving potential exposure to non-ionising radiation are included in a much larger group with slightly raised odds ratios[9]. The second reports a cluster of cases with parents employed at the same electronics firm where, although the estimated risk was high, no controls were studied[10].

Neuroblastoma

11   Three case-control studies have specifically reported on neuroblastoma and paternal exposure to electromagnetic fields[11-13]. The studies from Texas[11] and

| Study | Exposure group | Number of exposed | | Odds ratio[a] | 95% CI |
		Cases	Controls		
Wilkins and Koutras[5]	Electrical assembling, installing and repairing in structural work	19	9	2.7	1.2–6.1
	In machinery industry[b]	16	7	3.6	1.3–10.0
Nasca *et al*[6]	At birth				
	narrow definition[c]	15	18	1.70	0.80–3.59
	broad definition[c]	19	24	1.61	0.83–3.11
	At diagnosis				
	narrow definition[c]	11	18	1.28	0.56–2.91
	broad definition[c]	12	22	1.14	0.53–2.46
Johnson and Spitz[7]	All industry categories with potential exposure	25	31	1.64	0.96–2.82
	Computer and office machines manufacturing[b]	4	2	4.07	0.74–22.32
	All occupational categories with potential exposure	28	39	1.44	0.88–2.38
	Electricians[b]	7	4	3.52	1.02–12.08

TABLE 6.1
Nervous system tumours and paternal exposure to electromagnetic fields

Notes
(a)   After adjustment for factors mentioned in the text for the Wilkins and Koutras study.
(b)   Subgroup with highest odds ratio.
(c)   Narrow definition — electricians, electronics workers, power linemen and welders; broad definition — narrow plus electrical equipment repairmen and utility workers.

Philadelphia[13] were widely based investigations examining paternal occupation in general, whereas the one from Ohio[12] was initiated specifically to attempt to replicate the suggestion from the first study of an association between neuroblastoma and paternal exposure to electromagnetic fields. The third study reported specific analyses from a larger study to address this suggested association. The first two studies used birth certificates to obtain data on paternal occupation and industry, whereas the third used telephone interviews with the fathers where they were available to obtain complete job histories up to the end of the relevant pregnancy. In all three studies exposure classification methods were used as outlined above.

12   In the second study it was stated that the coding was not conducted blindly with respect to case or control status, but no mention of any such 'blindness' was made for the other two studies. In the first study possible confounding variables were not considered, whereas in the second adjustment was made for congenital anomalies, histories of stillbirths, birthweight, prematurity, birth order, parental ages and a job coding ambiguity score, and in the third one adjustment was made for educational level of the father and source of father's job data (father or proxy interview).

TABLE 6.2
*Case-control
studies of nervous
system tumours
and paternal
occupational
exposure to
electromagnetic
fields*

(a) *Definition and data on cases*

Cases	Study		
	Wilkins and Koutras[5]	Nasca *et al*[6]	Johnson and Spitz[7]
Number of cases	491	338	499
Type of cancer	Brain tumours	Central nervous system tumours	Nervous system tumours
Area	Ohio	53 New York State counties	Texas
Vital status	Deaths	Cases	Deaths
Source	Death certificates	Tumour register	Death certificates
Age group (years)	0–19	0–14	0–14
Calendar period of diagnosis	1959–78	1968–77	1964–80
Occupation source	Birth certificates	Telephone interviews with mothers using structured questionnaire for times of birth and diagnosis	Birth certificates
Industry source	Birth certificates		Birth certificates

(b) *Definition and data on controls*

Controls	Study		
	Wilkins and Koutras[5]	Nasca *et al*[6]	Johnson and Spitz[7]
Number of controls	491	676	998
Source	Ohio birth register	New York State birth register	Texas birth register
Selection	At random from case's year of birth	At random from case's year of birth	At random from case's year of birth
Occupation	Birth certificates	Telephone interviews with mothers using structured questionnaire for times of birth and diagnosis	Birth certificates
Industry	Birth certificates		Birth certificates
Controls per case	1	2	2
Matching	Year of birth, sex and race	Year of birth, sex and race	Year of birth, sex and race
Risk set ascertainment	No	No	No

(c) *Exposure assessment*

TABLE 6.2
(continued)

Exposure	Study		
	Wilkins and Koutras[5]	Nasca et al[6]	Johnson and Spitz[7]
Method	Birth certificate data	Ascertainment of job title, work and product description, employer at child's birth and diagnosis	Birth certificate data
Occupational coding	Dictionary of Occupational Titles	US Bureau of Census Classified Index of Industries and Occupations	Dictionary of Occupational Titles
Industrial coding	Standard Industrial Classification Manual	–	Standard Industrial Classification Manual
Electromagnetic field exposure classification	Hoar et al[1]	Based on occupational titles and previously published methods	Selected *a priori* from the occupational and industrial coding groups
Blindness to case/control	?	?	Yes
Confounders considered	Parental age, birth order, birthweight, sex, year of birth and rural or urban status of mother's county of residence at child's birth	Year of birth, sex and race	None

(d) *Comments on design and methodology*

Study		
Wilkins and Koutras[5]	Nasca et al[6]	Johnson and Spitz[7]
(1) Study limited to occupation/industry of father on child's birth certificate	(1) 85% interview response for case mothers and 70% for control mothers	(1) Study limited to occupation/industry of father on child's birth certificate
(2) Individual exposures only indirectly assessed through coding schemes	(2) Individual exposures only indirectly assessed through coding schemes	(2) Individual exposures only indirectly assessed through coding schemes
(3) Potential for other confounding exposures	(3) Potential for other confounding exposures	(3) Potential for other confounding exposures
(4) Multiple comparisons over a wide range of occupations and industries	(4) Multiple comparisons, but predefined grouping for potential exposure to electromagnetic fields	(4) As for Wilkins and Koutras[5], but primarily within electrical and electronics industry

TABLE 6.3
Results of case-control studies of nervous system tumours and paternal occupational exposure to electromagnetic fields

Study	Summary
Wilkins and Koutras[5]	Within structural work occupations (code 800—899) those classified to electrical assembling, installing and repairing (code 820—829) had an adjusted odds ratio for brain tumours of 2.7 (95% CI 1.2—6.1).
	Most of these cases and estimated risk were among workers classified to the machinery industry (code 07) with an adjusted odds ratio of 3.6 (95% CI 1.3—10.0).
Nasca *et al*[6]	Using predefined industrial and occupational categories with potential for exposure to electromagnetic fields the authors found for:
	(a) narrow exposure definition — odds ratios of 1.70 (95% CI 0.80—3.59) and 1.28 (95% CI 0.56—2.91) at birth and diagnosis, respectively;
	(b) broad exposure definition — odds ratios of 1.61 (95% CI 0.83—3.11) and 1.14 (95% CI 0.53—2.46) at birth and diagnosis, respectively.
Johnson and Spitz[7]	Using predefined industrial and occupational categories with potential for exposure to low frequency electromagnetic fields the authors found odds ratios for central nervous system tumours of 1.64 (95% CI 0.96—2.82) and 1.44 (95% CI 0.88—2.38), respectively.
	Some subgroups had higher or lower estimated risks.

13   The published results are summarised in Table 6.4. It can be seen that there is a wide range of odds ratios presented from 0 to 11.75 depending on which study and classification of potential exposure to electromagnetic fields is used. Most crucially it is noticeable that high odds ratios are found in the first study and much lower ones in the second and third. Thus the replication that was examined for as mentioned earlier was not found.

14   The groups 1 and 2 in Table 6.4 with potential electromagnetic field exposure were said by Spitz and Johnson[11] to be defined as by Wertheimer and Leeper[14], following the suggestion by the latter of a relationship between electric wiring configurations and childhood cancer. The most comparable classifications in the second study are said by the authors to be those of Lin *et al*[3]: (A + B) to group 1, and (A + B + C) to group 2. Although the former (A + B) has an odds ratio of 1.9, similar to the value of 2.14 found in the first study, the confidence interval is wide (0.4—9.7), whereas the latter (A + B + C) has an odds ratio of 0.7 compared with 2.13 in the first study. As in the first study, the third study reports results for groups 1 and 2 but with much lower odds ratios.

15   Aspects of design of the studies are given in Table 6.5; a summary of the results is presented in Table 6.6.

Other malignant neoplasms

16   A recent review[8] does not suggest any excesses of total childhood cancers or leukaemias and lymphomas or urinary system cancers among children with fathers in the electrical industry, although electromagnetic fields are not separately identified in the summary tables.

SUMMARY

17   There are limitations in the published studies, many of which are admitted in the original articles and are summarised by Savitz and Chen[8]. The main problem is exposure classification which has largely been carried out from paternal employment as recorded on birth certificate entries to give occupation and industry, and then using indirect linkage techniques to imply potential exposure to electromagnetic fields. In none of the studies have direct measurements of electromagnetic fields been made,

Study	Exposure group	Number of exposed Cases	Number of exposed Controls	Odds ratio[a]	95% CI
Spitz and Johnson[11]	Cluster 7[b] — Hseih *et al*[2]	10	6	3.17	1.13—8.89
	Potential electromagnetic field exposure				
	Group 1[c]	13	12	2.14	0.95—4.82
	Group 2[d]	17	16	2.13	1.05—4.35
	Electronics workers only	6	1	11.75	1.40—98.55
Wilkins and Hundley[12]	As Hoar *et al*[1]	0	5	0	—
	As Hseih *et al*[2]	24	92	1.1	0.5—2.3
	As Deapen and Henderson[4]	4	16	1.6	0.3—9.1
	As Lin *et al*[3]				
	definite (A)	1	3	—	—
	probable (B)	5	11	1.2	0.2—6.4
	possible (C)	13	68	0.5	0.2—1.2
	(A + B)	6	14	1.9	0.4—9.7
	(A + B + C)	19	82	0.7	0.3—1.5
Bunin *et al*[13]	Cluster 7[b] — Hseih *et al*[2]				
	preconception	3	10	0.3	0.05—1.2
	pregnancy	3	9	0.3	0.1—1.3
	Group 1[c]				
	preconception	9	7	1.3	0.4—4.1
	pregnancy	3	9	0.3	0.1—1.3
	Group 2[d]				
	preconception	14	14	1.0	0.4—2.3
	pregnancy	7	12	0.6	0.2—1.6

TABLE 6.4
Neuroblastoma and paternal exposure to electromagnetic fields

Notes
(a)   After adjustment for factors mentioned in text for the Wilkins and Hundley study[12].
(b)   Contains — among a number of other occupations — electricians, electrical and electronics workers.
(c)   Group 1 = electricians, electrical and electronics workers, linemen, welders and utility employees.
(d)   Group 2 = Group 1 plus electrical equipment salesmen and repairmen.

TABLE 6.5
Case-control studies of neuroblastoma and paternal occupational exposure to electromagnetic fields

(a) *Definition and data on cases*

Cases	Study		
	Spitz and Johnson[11]	Wilkins and Hundley[12]	Bunin *et al*[13]
Number of cases	157	101	104
Type of cancer	Neuroblastoma	Neuroblastoma	Neuroblastoma
Area	Texas	Columbus, Ohio State	Greater Philadelphia
Vital status	Deaths	Cases	Cases
Source	Death certificates	Tumour register	Tumour registers
Age group (years)	0—14	0—15	'Childhood'
Calendar period of diagnosis	1964—78	?	1970—79
Occupation source	Birth certificates	Birth certificates	Telephone interviews with fathers for complete occupational history
Industry source	Birth certificates	Birth certificates	

(b) *Definition and data on controls*

Controls	Study		
	Spitz and Johnson[11]	Wilkins and Hundley[12]	Bunin *et al*[13]
Number of controls	314	404	104
Source	Texas birth register	Ohio birth register	Telephone
Selection	At random from cases's year of birth	Two nearest each side of case's entry	Random digit dialling
Occupation	Birth certificates	Birth certificates	Telephone interviews with fathers for complete occupational history
Industry	Birth certificates	Birth certificates	
Controls per case	2	4	1
Matching	Year of birth	Year of birth, sex, race and mother's county of residence	Telephone area code and next five digits at date of diagnosis, race and date of birth (± 3 years)
Risk set ascertainment	No	No	Yes

(c) Exposure assessment

TABLE 6.5
(continued)

Exposure	Study		
	Spitz and Johnson[11]	Wilkins and Hundley[12]	Bunin et al [13]
Method	Birth certificate data	Birth certificate data	All jobs of 6 months or more prior to conception and all jobs during late pregnancy
Occupational coding	Hseih et al [2]	Hoar et al [1]	Hoar et al [1]
Industrial coding	Standard Industrial Classification Manual	Hoar et al [1]	Hoar et al [1]
Electromagnetic field exposure classification	Hseih et al [2] Wertheimer and Leeper[14]	Hoar et al [1] Hseih et al [2] Deapen and Henderson[4] Lin et al [3]	Hseih et al [2]
Blindness to case/control	?	No	?
Confounders considered	None	Congenital anomaly, history of stillbirth, birthweight, prematurity, birth order, parents' ages, job coding ambiguity score	Educational level and source of father's data (father or proxy interview)

(d) Comments on design and methodology

Study		
Spitz and Johnson[11]	Wilkins and Hundley[12]	Bunin et al [13]
(1) Study limited to occupation/industry of father on child's birth certificate	(1) Study limited to occupation/industry of father on child's birth certificate	(1) Childhood ages not given
(2) Individual exposures only indirectly assessed through coding schemes	(2) Individual exposures only indirectly assessed through coding schemes	(2) 70% response rate for cases and 57% for controls
(3) Potential for other confounding exposures	(3) Potential for other confounding exposures although some other factors are considered	(3) Individual exposures only indirectly assessed through coding schemes
(4) Multiple comparisons over a wide range of occupations and industries		(4) Potential for other confounding exposures although some other factors are considered

TABLE 6.6
*Results of
case-control
studies of
neuroblastoma and
paternal
occupational
exposure to
electromagnetic
fields*

Study	Summary
Spitz and Johnson[11]	From 30 occupational 'clusters' (Hseih *et al*[2]), one containing, among others, electricians, electric and electronics workers had an odds ratio for neuroblastoma of 3.17 (95% CI 1.13—8.89).
	Consequent reclassification of occupations considered to have electromagnetic field exposure gave:
	Group 1 narrow definition — electricians, electric and electronics workers, linemen, welders and utility employees, odds ratio of 2.14 (95% CI 0.95—4.82);
	Group 2 broad definition — group 1 plus electrical equipment salesmen and repairmen, odds ratio of 2.13 (95% CI 1.05—4.35).
Wilkins and Hundley[12]	Various published schemes were used to categorise potential for occupational exposure to electromagnetic fields and showed a range of odds ratios from 0.5 to 1.9 all with wide confidence intervals.
	The authors comment that the two schemes (A + B) and (A + B + C) they regard as similar to those used in the Spitz and Johnson study[11] (groups 1 and 2) gave odds ratios of 1.9 and 0.7.
Bunin *et al*[13]	The occupational cluster reported above by Spitz and Johnson had an odds ratio of 0.3 (95% CI 0.05—1.2) for preconception jobs and 0.3 (95% CI 0.1—1.3) for pregnancy jobs.
	Group 1 odds ratio of 1.3 (95% CI 0.4—4.1) for preconception, odds ratio of 0.3 (95% CI 0.1—1.3) for pregnancy.
	Group 2 odds ratio of 1.0 (95% CI 0.4—2.3) for preconception, odds ratio of 0.6 (95% CI 0.2—1.6) for pregnancy.

nor has information collected from birth certificates and interviews been validated by reference back to any original occupation or industry records. Additionally, consistent classification approaches have not always been used so that the potential for comparison and amalgamation of studies, which would be desirable because of the small numbers of cases, is limited.

18   There are three recent studies specifically of nervous system tumours that taken together are a little suggestive of a raised odds ratio in relation to fathers' occupational exposure to electromagnetic fields[5–7]. These include studies of what the authors describe as brain tumours, central nervous system tumours and nervous system tumours (including spinal cord tumours). The particular subgroups of workers identified as having the highest odds ratios differ, however, between each of the three studies. It is unclear whether other studies have found no relationship or have not examined their data for potential exposure to electromagnetic fields[8]. Overall the findings have to be seen as inconsistent, and there must be some concern that a reporting bias against negative results has occurred.

19   There are three recent studies specifically of neuroblastomas that taken together are not suggestive of any relation to fathers' potential occupational exposure to electromagnetic fields[11–13].

20 A review of the literature[8] does not suggest any relationships between other childhood cancers and potential paternal exposure to electromagnetic fields at work, although it is not clear whether in some studies relevant data were examined.

CONCLUSION

21 In no study have any measurements been made of the fathers' occupational exposure. With the weak evidence available, and given the low quality of exposure data in all of these studies, no definite conclusion for or against a relationship can be made.

REFERENCES

1   Hoar, S K, Morrison, A S, Cole, P, *et al.* An occupation and exposure linkage system for the study of occupational carcinogenesis. *J. Occup. Med.,* **22**, 722 (1980).

2   Hseih, C-C, Walker, A M, and Hoar, S K. Grouping occupations according to carcinogenic potential: Occupation clusters from an exposure linkage system. *Am. J. Epidemiol.,* **117**, 575 (1983).

3   Lin, R S, Dischinger, P C, Conde, J, *et al.* Occupational exposure to electromagnetic fields and the occurrence of brain tumours. *J. Occup. Med.,* **27**, 413 (1985).

4   Deapen, D M, and Henderson, B E. A case-control study of amyotrophic lateral sclerosis. *Am. J. Epidemiol.,* **123**, 790 (1986).

5   Wilkins, J R, and Koutras, R A. Paternal occupation and brain cancer in offspring: A mortality-based case-control study. *Am. J. Ind. Med.,* **14**, 299 (1988).

6   Nasca, P C, Baptiste, M S, MacCubbin, P A, Metzger, B B, Carlton, K, Greenwald, P, Armbrustmacher, V W, Earle, K M, and Waldman, J. An epidemiologic case-control study of central nervous system tumours in children and parental occupational exposures. *Am. J. Epidemiol.,* **128**, 1256 (1988).

7   Johnson, C C, and Spitz, M R. Childhood nervous system tumours: An assessment of risk associated with paternal occupations involving use, repair or manufacture of electrical and electronic equipment. *Int. J. Epidemiol.,* **18**, 756 (1989).

8   Savitz, D A, and Chen, J. Parental occupation and childhood cancer: Review of epidemiologic studies. *Environ. Health Perspect.,* **88**, 325 (1990).

9   Wilkins, J R, and Sinks, T. Parental occupation and intracranial neoplasms of childhood: Results of a case-control interview study. *Am. J. Epidemiol.,* **132**, 275 (1990).

10 Wilkins, J R, McLaughlin, J A, Sinks, T H, and Kosnik, E J. Parental occupation and intracranial neoplasms of childhood: Anecdotal evidence from a unique occupational cancer cluster. *Am. J. Ind. Med.,* **19**, 643 (1991).

11 Spitz, M R, and Johnson, C C. Neuroblastoma and paternal occupation: A case-control analysis. *Am. J. Epidemiol.,* **121**, 924 (1985).

12 Wilkins, J R, and Hundley, V D. Paternal occupational exposure to electromagnetic fields and neuroblastoma in offspring. *Am. J. Epidemiol.,* **131**, 995 (1990).

13 Bunin, G R, Ward, E, Kramer, S, Rhee, C A, and Meadows, A T. Neuroblastoma and parental occupation. *Am. J. Epidemiol.,* **131**, 776 (1990).

14 Wertheimer, N, and Leeper, E. Electrical wiring configurations and childhood cancer. *Am. J. Epidemiol.,* **109**, 273 (1979).

7 Exposure from Electrical Appliances and Cancer in Adults and Children

INTRODUCTION

1   Several epidemiological studies have been carried out that investigated cancer risk in relation to the use of electrical appliances. These dealt mainly with the use of electric blankets. Whilst the studies did not incorporate measurements of the associated electromagnetic (EM) fields, it has been estimated[1] that the use of an electric blanket would typically increase magnetic field exposure by 82% relative to background, with a likely range of 31–345%. The corresponding increase in electric field exposure relative to background was estimated to be 36%, with a likely range of 14–155%. Thus electric blanket use could approximately double magnetic field exposures in particular, although it was cautioned that little is known about peaks, harmonics or other features of this type of exposure[1].

2   It should be pointed out that there are two types of electric blanket, namely under-blanket and over-blanket. The former is used only to pre-heat the bed, whereas the latter is generally kept on during the night. The epidemiological studies have focused on the use of over-blankets.

3   Of the published epidemiological studies concerning electric blankets, four examined adult cancers. Two of these looked at leukaemia (acute non-lymphocytic[2] and myelogenous[1]) and the other two concerned testicular cancer[3] and post-menopausal breast cancer[4]. The risk of childhood cancer in relation to both *in-utero* and postnatal exposures from electric blankets and other electrical appliances was examined for all cancers[5] and leukaemia[6]. The last two papers were based on data collected at the same time as studies of residential EM field exposures[6,7], which are discussed in Chapter 4.

ADULT CANCERS

Studies undertaken

4   Details of the materials and methods for the four studies of adult cancers are summarised in Table 7.1. All of these were case-control studies. The cases were ascertained from cancer registrations in specific geographical areas in the USA over a 3–6 year period. For two of the studies[2,3], the controls were sampled by random digit dialling on the basis of telephone directories. In one study[1] a procedure was used that defined a sequence of dwellings on specified blocks close to the case's dwelling, and the aim was to interview the first matching resident in this sequence, so as to produce a close match on socioeconomic status. In the fourth study[4] controls were sampled from drivers' licence rosters for ages less than 65 years and from health care rosters for older ages. In none of the studies was it made clear whether the controls were resident in the study region at the time of the corresponding case's diagnosis, although one study[3] did state that the controls selected were in 1982–84, compared with diagnoses for the cases made during 1981–84.

5   In each of the studies the only information on electric blanket use was that obtained from interviews; no measurements of EM fields were made for the study subjects. The degree to which electric blanket use was characterised varied between studies. One study[2] examined simply whether or not the subject had ever used an electric blanket. However, three studies[1,3,4], whilst considering 'ever-use' over a particular period prior to diagnosis, also asked about the duration of use, as well as (in the first study) when regular use commenced and ended, or (in the latter two studies) the length of use per year. It was made clear in one study[1] that the interviewers were not blind to case-control status.

Results

6   The odds ratios associated with electric blanket use in the studies are summarised in Table 7.2, with further details given in Table 7.3. For leukaemias that are of acute non-lymphocytic type, the odds ratio quoted by Wertheimer and Leeper[8] based on the Severson *et al* study[2] is 1.6, compared with 0.9 from the Preston-Martin *et al* study[1]; neither differs significantly from unity. However, Severson *et al* pointed out that the slightly raised risk for electric blanket use in their study was confined to those subjects with an annual family income of less than \$15,000 (odds ratio (OR) = 2.40, 95% confidence interval (CI) 0.99–5.84), whereas the odds ratio for those with a higher family income was 1.01 (95% CI 0.53–1.94). As pointed out in Table 7.1(c), 41% of all cases fell within the lower income category, compared with 29% of controls. In view of the inconsistency of the odds ratio between income groups, Severson *et al*[9] stated that they were reticent to place any strong emphasis on these results.

7   For chronic myelogenous leukaemia, no association was found with ever having used electric blankets regularly up to 2 years prior to diagnosis, or with average duration of use[1]. For both testicular cancer[3] and post-menopausal breast cancer[4], no association was found with ever having used electric blankets up to 10 years before diagnosis, while the distribution of duration of use was similar for the cases and the controls.

CHILDHOOD CANCERS

Studies undertaken

8   Details of the data on cases and controls for the studies by Savitz *et al*[5] and London *et al*[6], as well as comments on the design and methodology, are given in Table 4.1 (p 58). Of particular note in the study of Savitz *et al*[7], based on the same cases and controls as for the 1990 paper[5], was the difference in the residential requirements for cases and controls which may have led to the controls being selected from the less-mobile section of the population.

9   The assessment of exposures from electrical appliances is summarised in Table 7.4. No measurements of EM fields were made; the exposure assessment was made solely on the basis of interviews with parents. Apart from electric blankets, information was requested on the use of several other electrical appliances including heated water beds, electric clocks, and hair dryers (by the child). Distinction was made between *in-utero* and postnatal exposures.

TABLE 7.1   Case-control studies of adult cancer and electric blanket use

(a)   Definition and data on cases

Cases	Study			
	Preston-Martin et al[1]	Severson et al[2]	Verreault et al[3]	Vena et al[4]
Number of cases	224	114	182	382
Type of cancer	Acute and chronic myelogenous leukaemia	Acute non-lymphocytic leukaemia	Testicular	Breast
Area	Los Angeles County	Western Washington State	Western Washington State	Western New York State
Vital status	All cases	All cases	All cases	All cases
Source	Cancer register	Cancer register	Cancer register	Hospital records
Age group (years)	20—69	20—79	20—69	41—85
Calendar period	1979—85	1981—84	1981—84	1987—89

TABLE 7.1 *(continued)*

(b) Definition and data on controls

Controls	Study			
	Preston-Martin et al[f]	Severson et al[p]	Verreault et al[β]	Vena et al[π]
Number of controls	224	133	658	439
Source	List of dwellings on neighbourhood blocks	Telephone directories, using random digit dialling	Telephone directories, using random digit dialling	Rosters of drivers' licences and the Health Care Financing Administration
Selection	Choose first in a sequence designed to give a close match on socioeconomic status	Eligible telephone responders	Eligible telephone responders	Random selection from rosters
Controls per case	1	Approximately 1	Approximately 3–4 (not matched individually)	Approximately 1
Matching	Sex, race, year of birth (within 5 years) and neighbourhood	Frequency matching by age and sex	—	Frequency matching by age
Risk set ascertainment	?	?	?	?

TABLE 7.1 *(continued)*

(c) Exposure assessment

Exposure	Study			
	Preston-Martin *et al*[1]	Severson *et al*[2]	Verreault *et al*[3]	Vena *et al*[4]
Method	Telephone interviews with study subjects	Face-to-face interviews with study subjects or next-of-kin	Telephone interviews with study subjects	Face-to-face interviews with study subjects
Classification of electric blanket use	Ever used regularly up to 2 years before diagnosis Average duration of use Period of first regular use Time since last regular use	Ever used	Ever used in 10 years before diagnosis Number of years of use Number of months used per year	Number of years use in the 10 years before diagnosis Frequency of use during season Mode of use, eg continuously throughout night
Blindness to case/control	No	?	?	?
Confounders considered	Bone marrow exposure from diagnostic radiography Work as welder Work on farm	Family income	Marital status Education	(i) Age, education (ii) Age, education plus Quetelet index and reproductive risk factors

116

TABLE 7.1 *(continued)*

(d) Comments on design and methodology

Study					
Preston-Martin *et al*[1]	Severson *et al*[2]	Verreault *et al*[3]	Vena *et al*[4]		
(1) Interviews completed for 61% of eligible cases. Number of replacement controls not given	(1) Interviews completed for 70% of eligible cases and 65% of eligible controls	(1) Interviews completed for 72% of eligible cases and 66% of eligible controls	(1) Interviews completed for 51% of eligible cases and 46% of eligible controls		
(2) Cases who died prior to interview were excluded	(2) 41% of the cases had a combined annual income of less than $15 000, compared with 29% of controls	(2) No measurements of electromagnetic field exposure, nor validation of electric blanket use	(2) No measurements of electromagnetic field exposure, nor validation of electric blanket use		
(3) No measurements of electromagnetic field exposure, nor validation of electric blanket use	(3) No measurements of electromagnetic field exposure, nor validation of electric blanket use	(3) No information requested on electric blanket use more than 10 years before diagnosis	(3) No information requested on electric blanket use more than 10 years before diagnosis		

117

Results

10   Table 7.5 shows unadjusted odds ratios associated with *in-utero* exposures; additional information is given in Table 7.6. For none of the electrical appliances or cancer types does the odds ratio (OR) differ from unity to a statistically significant extent. The only indication of a raised value is for brain cancer in relation to *in-utero* electric blanket exposure[5] (OR = 1.8, 95% CI 0.9–4.0). Stratification of the results for electric blanket use by annual *per caput* income (Table 7.7) indicates differences by income[5]. For total cancer and for leukaemia the only suggestion of a raised odds ratio is in the lower income group (annual income of less than $7000 *per caput*), whereas the odds ratio in the higher income group is close to unity. For brain cancer, however, the odds ratio is similar for the two income groups and the overall value, adjusted for income, is raised significantly (OR = 2.5, 95% CI 1.1–5.5). Further analysis with adjustment for income shows that the brain cancer odds ratio is highest at ages

TABLE 7.2 *(a)   Acute non-lymphocytic leukaemia*
Case-control studies of adult cancer and electric blanket use

Study	Controls	Cases	Odds ratio	95% CI
Severson et al[a]				
Use of electrically heated bed[b]				
never	70	46		
ever	62	64	1.6	0.9–2.4
Preston-Martin et al				
Electric blanket use up to 2 years previously				
never	75	76[c]		
ever	43	40[c]	0.9[d]	0.5–1.6

Notes
(a)   Quoted by Wertheimer and Leeper[8], based on data supplied by Severson *et al*[5].
(b)   Severson *et al*[5] stated that examination of the use of electric blankets, electric water heaters and electric mattress pads separately did not show any significant associations.
(c)   Acute myelogenous leukaemia.
(d)   Matched odds ratio.

(b)   Chronic myelogenous leukaemia

Study	Controls	Cases	Odds ratio	95% CI
Preston-Martin et al				
Electric blanket use up to 2 years previously				
no	68	70		
yes	42	38	0.8*	0.4–1.6

*Matched odds ratio.

0–4 years (OR = 3.7, 95% CI 1.2–11.1) and for electric blanket use in the first trimester (OR = 4.0, 95% CI 1.6–9.9).

11   Table 7.8 shows unadjusted odds ratios associated with postnatal exposures from electric blankets and other appliances. The odds ratios for leukaemia in relation to electric blanket use are raised in both studies, although individually neither differs to a statistically significant extent from unity (Savitz *et al*: OR = 1.5, 95% CI 0.5–5.1; London *et al*: OR = 7.0, 95% CI 0.86–122). As Savitz *et al* pointed out, childhood electric blanket use tended to be rare, so leading to instability in the point estimates of risk. The odds ratio for total cancer in relation to electric blanket use in this study is 1.5 (95% CI 0.6–3.4), while the corresponding odds ratio for brain cancer is 1.2 (95% CI 0.3–5.7). No results with adjustment for family income were quoted in the study, whilst it was stated that analyses by duration and magnitude of electric blanket use precluded definite results owning to small numbers. The only odds ratio in Table 7.8 that is significantly raised is that for leukaemia in relation to hair dryer use in the London *et al* study[6]. However, there is no overlap between the 95% confidence interval for the odds ratio in this study (ie 95% CI 1.42–6.32) and the corresponding interval from the Savitz *et al* study (ie 95% CI 0.2–1.3). Out of nine electrical appliances other than those in Table 7.8 that were studied solely by London *et al* (see Table 7.6), the leukaemia odds

(c)   Testicular cancer

TABLE 7.2
(continued)

Study	Controls	Cases	RR*	95% CI
Verreault et al				
Electric blanket use in previous 10 years				
never	446	125		
ever	212	57	1.0	0.7–1.4
Cumulative use (months)				
0	446	125		
1–24	123	30	0.9	0.5–1.3
25–120	89	27	1.2	0.7–1.9

*Rate ratio, adjusted for age in 10 year groups.

(d)   Breast cancer

Study	Controls	Cases	Odds ratio*	95% CI
Vena et al				
Electric blanket use in previous 10 years				
never	284	255		
ever	154	126	0.89	0.66–1.19

*Adjusted for age and education.

TABLE 7.3   Results of case-control studies of adult cancer and electric blanket use

Study	Summary
Preston-Martin et al[1]	Odds ratio associated with ever using electric blankets regularly up to 2 years prior to diagnosis was 0.9 (95% CI 0.5–1.6) for acute myeolgenous leukaemia (AML) and 0.8 (95% CI 0.4–1.6) for chronic myelogenous leukaemia (CML). Cases and controls did not differ significantly by average duration of use (AML: 8.5 years for cases. 7.0 years for controls: CML: 9.0 and 10.0 years, respectively). by year of first regular use (AML: 1971 against 1971: CML: 1970 against 1970). or by years since last regular use (AML: 3.2 against 4.1: CML: 2.7 against 2.8).
	Adjustments for bone marrow exposure for diagnostic radiography, having ever worked as a welder or having ever lived on a farm did not increase the association for electric blanket use.
Severson et al[2]	Odds ratio for acute non-lymphatic leukaemia associated with electric blanket use was 2.40 (95% CI 0.99–5.84) for those with a family income less than \$15 000 per year, and 1.01 (95% CI 0.53–1.94) for those with a higher income.
Verreault et al[3]	The odds ratio for testicular cancer associated with electric blanket use up to 10 years prior to diagnosis was 1.0 (95% CI 0.7–1.4). The odds ratio for seminoma germ cell tumours was slightly smaller (0.7: 95% CI 0.5–1.2) and that for other germ cell tumours slightly larger (1.4: 95% CI 0.9–2.3). Among those who had used electric blankets for more than 24 months in total, the odds ratios were 0.8 (95% CI 0.5–1.6) for seminomas. 1.8 (95% CI 0.9–3.6) for non-seminomas, and 1.2 (95% CI 0.7–1.9) for all testicular tumours.
	Additional adjustment for marital status and education did not materially alter the results.
Vena et al[4]	There was no indication of trends in the odds ratio according to number of years of use or frequency of use during season; the odds ratio for daily use relative to non-use was 0.97 (95% CI 0.70–1.35). By mode of use, the odds ratio for warming the bed only was 0.64 (95% CI 0.39–1.05). for using continuously throughout the night 1.31 (95% CI 0.88–1.95) and for fluctuating between these modes 0.64 (95% CI 0.40–1.05).
	Additional adjustment for Quetelet index and reproductive risk factors did not materially alter the results.

TABLE 7.4   *Case-control studies of childhood cancer and use of electrical appliances – exposure assessment*

Exposure	Study	
	Savitz et al[5]	London et al[b]
Method	Face-to-face interview with parents	Interview with mother
Observations	Use of electric blanket, heated water bed, and electric clock by the bed (both for mother and child) Use of heating pad (mother only) Use of hair dryer (child only)	Use by child of any of 13 electrical appliances, including electric blanket Use by mothers during pregnancy of electric blanket, water bed, bedroom air conditioner, electric fan and electric space heater
Classification of exposures	*In utero* Trimester and daily duration of use by mother during pregnancy *Postnatal* Ages at which use began and ended, number of months used per year, time used per day Also, setting of electric blanket/heated water bed use (high, medium, low)	*In utero* Ever used by mother in pregnancy *Postnatal* Regular use (at least once a week) or not
Blinding to case-control	?	?
Potential confounders considered	Child's sex, age at diagnosis, year of diagnosis Mother's age, smoking during pregnancy Father's education Family's *per caput* income Wire code at time of diagnosis	Social class, use of incense, use of indoor pesticide, occupation of father (but unclear whether these were studied)

ratio differed from unity at the 5% level only for use of black and white television (OR = 1.49, 95% CI 1.01−2.23), whereas by contrast the odds ratio for colour television was close to unity (OR = 1.06, 95% CI 0.66−1.74).

DISCUSSION OF ADULT AND CHILD STUDIES

12   A problem common to all of the above studies is the lack of electromagnetic field measurements. Whilst most of the above studies obtained information on the duration and timing of the use of electrical appliances, the data collected provide only an indirect measure of EM field exposures. Furthermore, it was not possible to validate the information on electrical appliance use obtained in interviews. Monson[10] suggested that such points illustrate the inherent difficulty of epidemiological research on low level exposures: "On the one hand, weak associations are unlikely to be observed with certainty because of random misclassification of exposure. On the other hand, bias in the estimate of past exposure may lead to weak positive associations in epidemiological data that do not reflect causation.". There is clearly a

TABLE 7.5
*Case-control
studies of
childhood cancer
and use of
electrical
appliances −
in-utero exposures*

Appliance	Savitz et al [5]				London et al [6]		
	Use		Odds		Discordant	Odds	
	No	Yes	ratio	95% CI	pairs	ratio	95% CI
Electric blanket							
Controls	175	31			19		
Total cancer	195	38	1.1	0.7−1.8			
Leukaemia	57	13	1.3	0.7−2.6	23	1.21	0.66−2.29
Brain cancer	34	11	1.8	0.9−4.0			
Other cancer	104	14	0.8*	0.4−1.5*			
Heated water bed							
Controls	182	24			21		
Total cancer	213	21	0.7	0.4−1.4			
Leukaemia	67	3	0.3	0.1−1.2	14	0.67	0.34−1.28
Brain cancer	42	3	0.5	0.2−2.0			
Other cancer	104	15	1.1*	0.6−2.2*			
Bedside electric clock							
Controls	57	149					
Total cancer	76	157	0.8	0.5−1.2			
Leukaemia	21	48	0.9	0.5−1.6	—		
Brain cancer	14	31	0.8	0.4−1.7			
Other cancer	41	78	0.7*	0.4−1.2*			
Heating pad							
Controls	182	24					
Total cancer	202	29	1.1	0.6−1.9			
Leukaemia	60	7	0.9	0.4−2.2	—		
Brain cancer	40	5	0.9	0.4−2.7			
Other cancer	102	17	1.3*	0.7−2.4*			

*Unmatched

TABLE 7.6 *Results of case-control studies of childhood cancer and use of electrical appliances*

Study	Summary
Savitz *et al*[5]	*In utero* In analyses of electric blanket use adjusted for annual *per caput* income (<$7000, $7000+), there was little indication of differences in odds ratios for any cancer type between high and low/medium blanket settings. There was a suggestion that the odds ratio was highest for use in the first trimester, particularly for brain cancer (OR = 4.0, 95% CI 1.6–9.9; based on 9 cases). There were also indications that the odds ratio was greatest for nightly duration of use in excess of 8 hours, but based on very few subjects (six in total with cancer and one control).
London *et al*[6]	*In utero* For none of bedroom air conditioner (OR = 0.91, 95% CI 0.51–1.66), electric fan (OR = 1.16, 95% CI 0.77–1.75) or electric space heater (OR = 1.18, 95% CI 0.62–2.32) was there an indication of an association with the leukaemia risk. *Postnatal* Apart from the appliances covered in Table 7.8, nine other appliances were studied. The odds ratios ranged from 6.0 (95% CI 0.72–105) for curling iron (based on six discordant pairs for use by case and one for use by control) to 0.54 (95% CI 0.21–1.25) for bedroom air conditioner; six of the odds ratios were greater than unity, two were less and one equalled unity. The odds ratio for black and white television was raised significantly (OR = 1.49, 95% CI 1.01–2.23), whilst that for colour television use was close to unity (OR = 1.06, 95% CI 0.66–1.74).

TABLE 7.7 *Case-control study of childhood cancer and use of electric blankets according to annual per caput income — in-utero exposures*[5]

Annual per caput income	Controls	Total cancer		Leukaemia		Brain cancer		Other cancers	
		Number	Odds ratio[a] (95% CI)	Number	Odds ratio[a] (95% CI)	Number	Odds ratio[a] (95% CI)	Number	Odds ratio[b] (95% CI)
<$7000									
Unexposed	111	131		41		27		63	
Exposed	11	20	1.5 (0.7–3.3)	9	2.2 (0.9–5.7)	7	2.6 (1.0–7.2)	4	0.6 (0.3–1.3)
$7000+									
Unexposed	60	56		12		6		38	
Exposed	18	13	0.8 (0.3–1.7)	4	1.1 (0.3–3.9)	4	2.2 (0.6–4.6)	5	0.4 (0.1–1.3)
All									
Unexposed	175	195		57		34		104	
Exposed	31	38	1.3[c] (0.7–2.2)	13	1.7[c] (0.8–3.6)	11	2.5[c] (1.1–5.5)	14	0.6 (0.4–1.0)

Notes
(a) Matched.
(b) Unmatched.
(c) Odds ratio adjusted for annual *per caput* income (<$7000, $7000+).

TABLE 7.8
*Case-control study
of childhood
cancer and use of
electrical
appliances —
postnatal
exposures*

Appliance	Savitz et al [5]				London et al [6]		
	Use		Odds		Discordant	Odds	
	No	Yes	ratio	95% CI	pairs	ratio	95% CI
Electric blanket							
Controls	208	8			1		
Total cancer	231	13	1.5	0.6–3.4			
Leukaemia	69	4	1.5	0.5–5.1	7	7.00	0.86–122
Brain cancer	45	2	1.2	0.3–5.7			
Other cancer	117	7	1.6*	0.6–4.2*			
Heated water bed							
Controls	203	13			12		
Total cancer	233	11	0.7	0.3–1.7			
Leukaemia	70	3	0.7	0.2–2.5	12	1.00	0.45–2.29
Brain cancer	46	1	0.3	0.1–2.7			
Other cancer	117	7	0.9*	0.4–2.4*			
Bedside electric clock							
Controls	187	29			46		
Total cancer	202	42	1.3	0.8–2.2			
Leukaemia	60	13	1.4	0.7–2.9	61	1.33	0.90–1.97
Brain cancer	40	7	1.1	0.5–2.8			
Other cancer	102	22	1.4*	0.8–2.5*			
Hair dryer							
Controls	181	35			11		
Total cancer	212	32	0.8	0.5–1.3			
Leukaemia	66	7	0.5	0.2–1.3	31	2.82	1.42–6.32
Brain cancer	42	5	0.6	0.3–1.7			
Other cancer	104	20	1.0*	0.6–1.8*			

*Unmatched

need for better data on EM field exposures, preferably collected objectively on an individual basis, for epidemiological studies in this area. Even though the estimates quoted by Preston-Martin et al[1] indicate that electric blanket use may make a significant contribution to mean magnetic field exposure, little is known about peaks and other features of such exposures.

13   In each of the studies the proportion of eligible study subjects for whom interviews were completed was low. This ranged from 51% of eligible cases in the study by Vena et al[4] to 72% in that by Verreault et al[3], and from 46% of eligible controls in the Vena et al study to 80% in the Savitz et al study[5] (the number of replacement controls in the Preston-Martin et al study[1] was not stated). Furthermore, there was some suggestion of differences in response rates between cases and controls; for example, 71% and 80%, respectively, in the Savitz et al study. The low response rates raise considerable doubts as to the quality of the data on potential exposures.

14   For those who did respond to the request for an interview, there is the question of whether recall of electrical appliance use is biased by disease status. If many questions were asked in the interview, about not only electrical appliance use but also other exposures, then the differential recall for any one appliance might be small. However,

recall bias might not be small if there had been publicity on claimed associations beforehand or if the investigators had focused on one particular appliance in the interview. There is also the possibility that the response of surrogates differs from that of the study subjects. Whilst three of the adult studies[1,3,4] and the child studies based on *in-utero* exposures involved interviews with those who had (or had not) been using the appliances (the mothers in the case of *in-utero* exposures), the child studies based on postnatal exposures involved interviews with the parents rather than the children.

15   In one study[2] there was another problem in that case interviews were mostly performed with next-of-kin, whereas controls themselves were generally interviewed. One study[1] avoided this problem by being restricted to living subjects; while the authors thought their results may not be relevant for rapidly fatal cases of leukaemia, it seems unlikely that the exclusion of dead subjects would have introduced bias.

16   The results from the Severson *et al*[2] and Savitz *et al*[5] studies subdivided by income illustrate differences between the case and control series. For adult leukaemia in the Severson *et al* study and for total cancer and leukaemia in childhood based on *in-utero* exposures in the Savitz *et al* study, the odds ratio for electric blanket use is raised in the low income group but close to unity in the high income group. As mentioned in Chapter 4, in the Savitz *et al* study the recruitment of controls who had been living in the same region as the case subjects when the latter were diagnosed several years previously is likely to have led to controls being drawn from the less-mobile section of the population. For the Severson *et al* study, however, the controls were recruited over approximately the same time period as the case subjects were diagnosed, although it was not stated whether controls were 'at risk' at precisely the same time. However, for both studies the controls were recruited by random digit dialling based on telephone directories; this may have led to the smaller proportion of low income subjects among the control series than the case series (29% and 41%, respectively). In the Preston-Martin *et al* study[1], by contrast, the controls were selected from a list of dwellings near the corresponding case address and matched on socioeconomic status. In the Verreault *et al* study[3], for which the controls were selected by random digit dialling, adjustment by education was said not to have materially altered the results. However, the results from adjusting for social class in the London *et al* study[6] (which was based on random digit dialling) were not stated. The controls in the Vena *et al* study[4] were selected from driving licence and health care rosters, and adjustments for education were made in the analysis.

17   Even though there may be a deficit of low income controls in the Savitz *et al*[5] and Severson *et al*[2] studies, this does not by itself explain the apparent association with electric blankets in the low income group alone. One possibility might be that differences between case and control subjects in recalling electrical appliance use are greater for low than high income groups. Alternatively, since electrical appliance use would be expected to vary according to income, it may be that a simple dichotomy for income is not sufficient to remove income-based differences in both electrical appliance use and in the exclusion of potential controls.

18   In view of the problems concerning low income controls in these two studies, more reliance might be placed upon the results for the high income groups. For adult leukaemia in the Severson *et al* study and for total cancer and leukaemia in childhood

based on *in-utero* exposures in the Savitz *et al* study, the corresponding odds ratios (1.0, 0.8 and 1.1, respectively, each with 95% CIs including unity) do not suggest any elevated risk associated with electric blanket use. However, there is some indication of a raised odds ratio for brain cancer in the high income group in the Savitz *et al* study based on *in-utero* exposures from electric blankets (OR = 2.2, 95% CI 0.6–8.6). This odds ratio is similar to the corresponding value in the low income group. Further analyses adjusted for income showed that the odds ratio from brain cancer was highest at ages less than 5 years, for exposures in the first trimester, and increased with increasing nightly duration of use (although the last result was based on small numbers). However, there did not appear to be any difference between the odds ratios associated with high and low/medium blanket settings.

19   The results given by Savitz *et al* for postnatal electric blanket use and for exposures (both *in-utero* and postnatal) from heated water beds, bedside electric clocks and hair dryers do not indicate any excess risks (Tables 7.5 and 7.8). However, these results were neither adjusted for income, nor given separately by income group. The London *et al* study gave a high but unstable estimate of the odds ratio for leukaemia in relation to postnatal electric blanket use, based on seven case-control pairs for which only the leukaemic child used an electric blanket as opposed to one pair for which use was confined to the control. In the Savitz *et al* study the numbers were also small; only four leukaemic children used an electric blanket. The results for postnatal hair dryer use in these two studies are statistically incompatible at the 5% level, with the London *et al* but not the Savitz *et al* study suggesting raised risks of leukaemia. This may well represent bias in at least one of these studies. Out of the nine electrical appliances whose postnatal use was studied by London *et al* but not by Savitz *et al*, the only one for which the leukaemia risk was raised significantly at the 5% level was black and white television. This could well be a chance finding arising from examining many appliances. Alternatively, taking account of the absence of a raised risk for colour television use and the income-based differences in the use of the two types of television, this might be due to a deficit of low income controls in the London *et al* study.

20   The studies by Preston-Martin *et al*[1], Verreault *et al*[3] and Vena *et al*[4], along with that by Severson *et al*[2] for high income subjects, are consistent in not demonstrating any raised risk of adult cancer in relation to electric blanket use. Apart from the caveats mentioned earlier, there is the question of whether the time period over which electric blanket use was studied, was relevant. Preston-Martin *et al* disregarded exposures in the 2 years before diagnosis of myelogenous leukaemia. Verreault *et al* and Vena *et al* disregarded exposures more than 10 years before diagnosis of testicular and breast cancer, respectively, whereas Severson *et al* considered exposures irrespective of when they had been received in their study of acute non-lymphocytic leukaemia. In the absence of information on the form of any biological mechanism, it is difficult to decide which time period is relevant. However, the uniformity of the findings based on studies with different choices of time periods does not suggest that this factor is of crucial importance.

21   The power of the studies to detect any excess risk is dependent on the degree to which the electrical appliances are used. Preston-Martin *et al* queried whether their

findings for leukaemia in relation to electric blanket use in Los Angeles County could be generalised to areas with longer and colder winters. However, the results from Severson *et al* for high income subjects in Washington County — further north in the USA — were fairly similar to those of Preston-Martin *et al.* The examination by Savitz *et al* and London *et al* of childhood cancer in relation to postnatal electric blanket and heated water bed use was affected by the small proportion of children who used these appliances: among controls in the former study, only 4% used electric blankets and 6% used heated water beds. However, the proportion of children with *in-utero* electric blanket exposures was higher: 23% among high income controls in the Savitz *et al* study and 9% among low income controls. Consequently, the power to detect any risk associated with *in-utero* exposures should be greater than that for postnatal exposures.

SUMMARY

Adult cancers

22   The four published case-control studies of adult cancers do not show any association between the use of electric blankets and the risk of leukaemia, testicular cancer or breast cancer. However, these studies were limited by the absence of electromagnetic field measurements and the low proportion of eligible study subjects for whom interviews were completed.

Childhood cancers

23   There is a slight suggestion from a case-control study of all childhood cancers of a raised risk of brain cancer associated with exposure *in utero* (but not postnatally) from electric blankets. This study did not show any associations for other cancer types or for the use of other electrical appliances. Another case-control study that examined solely leukaemia gave a non-significant excess in relation to postnatal (but not *in-utero*) electric blanket exposures, but based on very small numbers.

24   However, there are four limitations to these studies.

(a)   No electromagnetic field measurements were made, and exposures were assessed on the basis of information collected in interviews with parents. This raises the possibility of bias in the recall of use.

(b)   The proportion of potential study subjects for whom interviews were completed was low.

(c)   There appear to have been biases in the selection of controls for at least one of the studies.

(d)   There is a problem of multiple significance testing when examining the use of many different electrical appliances.

CONCLUSION

25   In view of the possibility of bias, it is concluded that the childhood cancer studies are incapable of interpretation. No association with electrical appliance use was found in studies of adult cancer.

REFERENCES

1   Preston-Martin, S, Peters, J M, Yu, M C, Garabrant, D H, and Bowman, J D. Myelogenous leukaemia and electric blanket use. *Bioelectromagnetics,* **9**, 207 (1988).

2   Severson, R K, Stevens, R G, Kaune, W T, Thomas, D B, Heuser, L, Davis, S, and Sever, L E. Acute nonlymphocytic leukaemia and residential exposure to power frequency magnetic fields. *Am. J. Epidemiol.,* **128**, 10 (1988).

3   Verreault, R, Weiss, N S, Hollenbach, K A, Strader, C H, and Daling, J R. Use of electric blankets and risk of testicular cancer. *Am. J. Epidemiol.,* **131**, 759 (1990).

4   Vena, J E, Graham, S, Hellman, R, Swanson, M, and Brasure, J. Use of electric blankets and risk of postmenopausal breast cancer. *Am. J. Epidemiol.,* **134**, 180 (1991).

5   Savitz, D A, John, E M, and Kleckner, R C. Magnetic field exposure from electric appliances and childhood cancer. *Am. J. Epidemiol.,* **131**, 763 (1990).

6   London, S J, Thomas, D C, Bowman, J D, Sobel, E, Cheng, T-C, and Peters, J M. Exposure of residential electric and magnetic fields and risk of childhood leukaemia. *Am. J. Epidemiol.,* **134**, 923 (1991).

7   Savitz, D A, Wachtel, H, Barnes, F A, John, E M, and Tvrdik, J G. Case-control study of childhood cancer and exposure to 60-Hz magnetic fields. *Am. J. Epidemiol.,* **128**, 21 (1988).

8   Wertheimer, N, and Leeper, E. *Re* 'Acute nonlymphocytic leukaemia and residential exposure to power frequency magnetic fields'. *Am. J. Epidemiol.,* **130**, 423 (1989).

9   Severson, R K, Stevens, R G, Davis, S, Thomas, D, Heuser, L, and Sever, L E. Reply to letter from N Wertheimer and E Leeper. *Am. J. Epidemiol.,* **130**, 425 (1989).

10 Monson, R R. Editorial: Epidemiology and exposure to electromagnetic fields. *Am. J. Epidemiol.,* **131**, 774 (1990).

8 Conclusions

1 Interpretation of the findings that have been examined is not easy and is made even more difficult by the realisation that an incorrect assessment could have serious medical and socioeconomic implications. In reaching its conclusions the Advisory Group has, however, sought to base them solely on scientific considerations.

2 The experimental findings are, unfortunately, not very helpful. It cannot be concluded either that electromagnetic fields have no effect on the physiology of cells, even if the fields are weak, or that they produce effects that would, in other circumstances, be regarded as suggestive of potential carcinogenicity. In general, the available experimental evidence weighs against electromagnetic fields acting directly to damage cellular DNA, implying that these fields may not be capable of initiating cancer in a manner that parallels that of ionising radiation and many chemical agents. The results of some whole animal and cellular studies suggest the possibility that electromagnetic fields might act as co-carcinogens or tumour promoters but, taken overall, the data are inconclusive.

3 Animal studies conducted at frequencies above about 100 kHz have provided some evidence for effects on tumour incidence but, for some data, indirect temperature-mediated effects could not be excluded. In other studies, an increased rate of *in-vitro* malignant transformation was demonstrated in a chromosomally abnormal cell line but the *in-vivo* implications of these findings remain uncertain. No epidemiological study has been carried out that would indicate whether exposure to such fields causes an increased risk of cancer in humans. It can be concluded only that the evidence for a co-carcinogenic or tumour promoting effect of such relatively high frequency fields is not convincing.

4 At lower frequencies, the experimental evidence provides no reason to suggest that a carcinogenic effect of any sort is at all likely except possibly for a small risk attributable to an effect on the secretion of melatonin. Some human observations have, however, been interpreted as implying that a variety of carcinogenic hazards might result from exposure at work, or, in relation to childhood cancers, exposure at home from proximity to power lines or the use of some electrical appliances, or exposure of a parent at work before the child was conceived.

5 The greatest concern has been caused by the reports of an excess of cancer in children who have been exposed to above-average levels of electromagnetic fields by virtue of their place of residence. Seven studies have been reported since the appearance of the first in 1979, all of the case-control type in which comparisons have been made between the proximity of various sources of electromagnetic fields to the places of residence of children who had or who had not developed cancer. The results have been variable, but, taken at face value, they appear to provide some weak evidence in support of the postulated association which is less weak for brain cancer than for leukaemia and less weak when exposure is estimated from the local 'wire configurations' than from proximity to sources of electromagnetic fields or from measurements in the home. This evidence is, however, difficult to accept as the

methodology of the most important studies failed to obtain sets of control data that could be confidently regarded as representative of the populations from which the affected children were drawn. The major positive results may in consequence be artefacts of the method of enquiry.

6   Few data are available that bear on the possible effect of residential exposure on the risk of cancer in adults and these do not suggest the existence of any hazard.

7   The greatest amount of data relates to putative hazards associated with exposure at work. Many studies of several specific types of cancer have been carried out with results varying from a deficiency of cases to an excess; none has provided evidence of a quantitative relationship between risk and level of exposure. Review of 29 studies with informative data for leukaemia leads to the conclusion that a tendency for the selective publication of results that suggest an increased risk is perhaps the most likely explanation of the very small overall excess incidence from the disease that the totality of the data implies. This seems less likely to be the explanation for the somewhat greater, but still small, excess of brain cancer in the 22 studies that have been reviewed and, in this case, the balance of evidence weighs weakly in favour of the existence of an occupational hazard in association with at least some types of electrical and electronic work. Whether the hazard, if one exists, is due to exposure to electromagnetic fields or to some chemical associated with the work is impossible to decide.

8   Few reports have been published relating other types of cancer to occupational exposure to electromagnetic fields. Those that have reported excess risks of breast cancer in men do not allow any conclusions to be drawn, but the experimental evidence is suggestive enough to require further investigation of the possibility that electromagnetic fields could have such an effect. Those reports relating to other cancers have been based on small numbers and the most reasonable explanation of the findings to date is that they are the sort of chance observations that will almost certainly be made when the risks of many types of cancer are examined in many studies.

9   Six case-control studies have reported on the occupations of the fathers of children with central nervous system tumours or neuroblastomas and have estimated risks for the development of these diseases if the fathers had had potential for occupational exposure to electromagnetic fields at the time of the children's birth. Those studies of children with neuroblastomas are not suggestive of any relationship to potential paternal exposure, while those of children with central nervous system tumours could be. The subgroups of workers associated with the highest risks differ, however, between each of the studies and it is unclear whether similar relationships have not been sought by the many other studies of children with central nervous system tumours or whether they have been sought, not found, and not referred to. On the present evidence no definite conclusion for or against the existence of a relationship can be reached.

10   Six studies have reported on the relationship between cancer and the use of electrical appliances. Two studies of childhood cancer suggested some associations with the use of electric blankets, but the possibility of recall bias and uncertainty about the representative nature of the controls mean that these results are incapable of interpretation. Four studies of adult cancer did not show any relationship with electrical appliance use.

11   In summary, the epidemiological findings that have been reviewed provide no firm evidence of the existence of a carcinogenic hazard from exposure of paternal gonads, the fetus, children, or adults to the extremely low frequency electromagnetic fields that might be associated with residence near major sources of electricity supply, the use of electrical appliances, or work in the electrical, electronic, and telecommunications industries. Much of the evidence that has been cited is inconsistent, or derives from studies that have been inadequately controlled, and some is likely to have been distorted by bias against the reporting or publishing of negative results. The only finding that is at all notable is the consistency with which the least weak evidence relates to a small risk of brain tumours. This consistency is, however, less impressive than might appear as brain tumours in childhood and adult life are different in origin, arising from different types of cell.

12   In the absence of any unambiguous experimental evidence to suggest that exposure to these electromagnetic fields is likely to be carcinogenic, in the broadest sense of the term, the findings to date can be regarded only as sufficient to justify formulating a hypothesis for testing by further investigation.

9 Recommendations for Research

EXPERIMENTAL STUDIES

1   The Advisory Group recognises that the current paucity of fundamental knowledge on the biological effects of low level electromagnetic fields and the multitude of experimental variables involved make it difficult to propose a specific programme of research aimed towards resolving possible carcinogenic effects. In general, however, it was thought that further directed work on fundamental biophysical interactions and on possible promotional/co-carcinogenic effects of electromagnetic fields should be emphasised.

2   A feature of the current experimental database is the difficulty experienced in reproducing some apparent biological effects and a lack of coherence between different investigations of similar biological endpoints. The Advisory Group suggests that more emphasis is needed on the consolidation of 'positive' findings and the formulation of the testable hypotheses necessary for the whole field to progress beyond the largely phenomenological position it currently occupies.

3   The following set of research areas, whilst not comprehensive, serves to highlight further studies that should be considered.

Biophysical studies

4   While some biophysical models of possible cellular and tissue interactions have been formulated there is need for further theoretical consideration of how electromagnetic fields might operate at the biomolecular level. Here, the possibilities of long-range co-operative interactions and ionic resonance effects on the cell membrane leading to physiological changes within and between cells have been suggested. It was also considered important to explore further the possibility that specific frequency and amplitude windows exist for the induction of biological effects. If these could be unambiguously shown to exist then it might be necessary to revise the conventional view that a simple relationship should exist between the level of electromagnetic field exposure and potential biological effect. In addition, since electromagnetic fields are known to affect chemical radical-mediated reactions in simple organic solutions[1,2], it would be valuable to know whether such effects modulate cellular biochemical reactions involving radical intermediates, particularly those thought to play a role in tumour promotion[3]. In general, however, current theoretical models are not sufficiently developed or lack convincing experimental support. A major potential benefit of experimentally supported theoretical models is that they may provide guidance on the appropriate exposure conditions under which further experimental and epidemiological evidence of electromagnetic field effects might be sought.

Studies on cell membrane function and gene expression

5   Theoretical and some experimental studies point towards the cell membrane as a possible target for electromagnetic fields to affect. Mammalian cells interact with their environment through specific membrane protein receptors. Such receptors allow the

transduction of extracellular signals from growth factors and hormones into the cytoplasm where they interact with biochemical pathways known to be involved in both tumour promotion and the activation of tumour-associated genes. In addition to this, some tumour promoters are now believed to interfere with cell-to-cell communications through specialised membrane structures thus terminating the signals that may normally suppress pre-neoplastic cell proliferation[4]. Studies on electromagnetic field effects in these crucial areas of cell physiology and growth response may yield valuable information on whether these fields have biophysical properties consistent with a tumour promotion mechanism.

Cell transformation studies

6   Many of the currently used cell transformation systems are based on grossly abnormal mammalian cell lines and may not provide a reliable guide to *in-vivo* carcinogenic potential. It is therefore recommended that studies on possible electromagnetic field effects be extended to include newly developing transformation systems based on more normal cultured mammalian cells and grafted tissue explants[5] where more directly relevant data may be expected.

Whole animal experiments

7   It was felt that large-scale animal studies would be necessary to explore further possible promotional/co-carcinogenic effects and while there is a paucity of quantitatively reliable animal models of tumour promotion it is suggested that a limited number of such studies should be considered. A murine model of skin carcinogenesis[6] might offer the best immediate opportunities but animal models of leukaemogenesis and brain tumorigenesis might also be sought. In addition, the experimental studies revealing a possible association between electromagnetic field exposure, melatonin synthesis and breast cancer were considered to be potentially important; further research in this area is also recommended.

8   In conclusion, the Advisory Group believes that, while existing data are inconclusive, further experimental studies can play a significant role in resolving current uncertainties on the possible association between electromagnetic fields and carcinogenesis and, in this respect, provide some guidance for the design and interpretation of more definitive epidemiological studies.

EPIDEMIOLOGICAL STUDIES

9   Evidence strong enough to justify the conclusion that exposure to greater than normal electromagnetic fields can cause cancer in humans or to allow the hypothesis to be rejected is unlikely to be obtained without much high quality epidemiological research that includes appropriate exposure measurements. Two approaches are most likely to be fruitful: study of cohorts of workers occupationally exposed to different fields and case-control study of the history of children who develop the disease in comparison with that of unaffected controls.

10   Interest in potential occupational hazards focuses primarily on the risk of developing brain cancer and leukaemia. Both are rare diseases, large numbers of exposed workers will need to be studied, and detailed proposals for further research

cannot be made until more information is obtained about the numbers of workers in different industries who are likely to have been materially exposed in the past or are likely to be so exposed in the future. The immediate need is, therefore, for surveys to be carried out in the industries that are suspected of causing exposure substantially above normal to determine the characteristics of personal exposures and the number of workers likely to be exposed to different levels and to different extents.

11   Children's cancers have the advantage from the point of view of epidemiological investigation that past exposures of the children relevant to the causation of the disease can have been only brief and, in most cases, it is possible to identify and make measurements in all the locations in which the children have lived.

12   Informative studies will need to provide objective observations about a group of control children that constitutes a truly representative sample of the population from which the affected children are drawn. At the same time, information will need to be obtained about the extent to which the children have been exposed to other suspected aetiological agents. A study of this sort is complex and expensive, but it could be carried out in a reasonable time more easily in the United Kingdom than in most other countries — for not only is the population of children sufficiently large to provide enough cases for the detection of quite a small hazard within a few years, but the structure of the national records also provides a suitable sampling base from which a satisfactory control group can be readily obtained.

13   It is recommended that research along both these lines should be undertaken as soon as practicable.

REFERENCES

1   McLaughlan, K A, and Steiner, U E. The spin correlated radical pair as a reaction intermediate. *Mol. Phys.,* **73**, 241 (1991).

2   Steiner, U E, and Ulrich, E. Magnetic field effects in chemical kinetics and related phenomena. *Chem. Rev.,* **89**, 51 (1989).

3   Cerutti, P A. Prooxidant states and tumour promotion. *Science,* **227**, 375 (1985).

4   Trosko, J E, Chang, C C, Madhukar, B V, and Klaunig J E. Chemical, oncogene and growth factor inhibition of gap junction intercellular communication: An integrative hypothesis of carcinogenesis. *Pathobiology,* **58**, 265 (1990).

5   Chadwick, K, Barnhart, B, and Seymour, C (eds). *Cell Transformation Systems and Radiation Induced Cancer in Man.* Bristol, Adam Hilger (1989).

6   Bowden, G T, Jaffe, D, and Andrews, K. Biological and molecular aspects of radiation carcinogenesis in mouse skin. *Radiat. Res.,* **121**, 235 (1990).

Glossary

TERMS ASSOCIATED WITH ELECTROMAGNETIC FIELDS

antenna   a device designed to radiate or receive electromagnetic energy.

decibel (dB)   a measure of the increase or decrease in power at two points (1,2) expressed in logarithmic form; gain (dB) $= 10 \log_{10}(P_2/P_1)$.

dielectric   a class of materials that act as electric insulators.

dipole   a centre fed open antenna excited in such a way that a standing wave of current is symmetrical about the midpoint of the antenna.

directivity   that property of an antenna by virtue of which it radiates more strongly in some directions than in others.

dosimetry   the measurement of the absorbed dose or dose rate by an object in a radiofrequency field.

effective radiated power (ERP)   the power supplied to the antenna multiplied by the gain of the antenna in that direction relative to a half-wave dipole.

electric field strength (E)   the force on a stationary unit positive charge at a point in an electric field. The magnitude of the electric field vector (unit V m^{-1}).

far field   the region at a distance greater than a wavelength from a source where the electric and magnetic field components lie transverse to each other and to the direction of propagation; the shape of the field is independent of distance and is also described as plane wave. For antennas where the wavelength is smaller than the largest dimension, D, the approximate distance at which far-field conditions would be satisfied is given by $2D^2/\lambda$.

gain   the ratio, usually expressed in decibels, of the power that would have to be supplied to a reference antenna to the power supplied to the antenna being considered so that they produce the same field strength at the same distance in the same direction.

harmonics   multiples of the fundamental frequency used for a particular source, eg 50 Hz harmonics are 100 Hz, 150 Hz, 200 Hz, etc.

Helmholtz coils   arrangement of two current carrying coils to produce a uniform magnetic field distribution between the coils.

hertz (Hz)   one cycle per second.

impedance (of free space)   the ratio of electric to magnetic field strength of an electromagnetic wave. In free space the value is 377 Ω.

isotropic (radiator)   having the same properties in all directions.

lobe   a part of the antenna radiation pattern between adjacent minima.

near field   a region close to a source or antenna where electric and magnetic fields do not have the plane-wave characteristics of far fields; at distances less than about a half wavelength from the antenna, the near field is described as *reactive* and indicates a region containing most of the stored energy associated with the field. If the antenna is large compared to the wavelength, constructive and destructive interference effects can arise and the region is termed the *interference* near field.

permeability (μ)   the quantity which, when multiplied by the magnetic field strength, gives the magnetic flux density. It indicates the degree of magnetisation in a medium when a magnetic field is applied.

permittivity (ε)   the quantity which, when multiplied by the electric field strength, gives the electric flux density. It indicates the degree of polarisation in a medium when an electric field is applied.

plane wave   a wave such that the corresponding physical quantities are uniform in any plane perpendicular to a fixed direction.

power (flux) density (S)   the power crossing unit area normal to the direction of wave propagation.

Poynting vector   a vector, the flux of which through any surface represents the instantaneous electromagnetic power transmitted through this surface (synonymous with power flux density).

root mean square (RMS)   certain electrical effects are proportional to the square root of the mean value of the square of a periodic function; this is known as the effective value or root mean square value.

wavelength (λ)   the distance between two successive points of a periodic wave in the direction of propagation, in which the oscillation has the same phase.

EPIDEMIOLOGICAL TERMS

case-control study   an investigation into the extent to which a group of persons with a specific disease (the cases) and comparable persons who do not have the disease (the controls) differ with respect to exposure to putative risk factors.

chi-square (χ^2) statistic   a statistic to test for any association between disease risk and a measure of exposure. For a case-control study, this is based on the classification of cases and controls by level of exposure. To test for any association, the statistic should be compared with the χ^2 distribution on the appropriate number of degrees of freedom. To adjust for confounding factors, see 'Mantel-Haenszel χ^2 statistic'.

cohort study   an investigation involving the identification of a group of individuals (the cohort) about whom certain exposure information is collected, and the ascertainment of the occurrence of diseases at later times. For each individual, information on prior exposures can be related to subsequent disease experience.

confidence interval (CI)   an interval calculated from data when making inferences about an unknown parameter. In hypothetical repetitions of the study, the interval will include the parameter in question on a specified percentage of occasions (eg 95% for a 95% confidence interval).

discordant pair   a pairing of a diseased case and a matched control for which the case and the control differ in their exposure to a given factor.

Mantel-Haenszel χ^2 statistic   a statistic to test for any association between disease risk and a dichotomous exposure measure in the presence of potential confounding factors. It is calculated by combining results from a series of 2×2 tables, corresponding to the classification of cases and controls by exposure status within each of a number of strata. These strata are defined so that, ideally, the data within each stratum are homogeneous with respect to the potential confounding factors. In order to test for any association between exposure and disease, this statistic should be compared with the χ^2 distribution on one degree on freedom.

matched odds ratio   the odds ratio *(see below)* calculated on the basis of the comparison of cases and controls that are matched with respect to potential confounding factors.

odds ratio   the ratio of the odds of disease occurrence in a group with exposure to a factor to that in an unexposed group; within each group, the odds are the ratio of the numbers of diseased and non-diseased individuals.

proportional mortality ratio (PMR)   the ratio of the fraction of deaths due to a particular cause in a cohort to the corresponding fraction in a general population, adjusted with respect to age (and sex if relevant) on the basis of the distribution of deaths from all causes in the cohort. PMR is often expressed as a percentage, ie a PMR of 100 indicates that proportionate mortality is the same in the cohort and the general population.

relative risk   the ratio of the disease rate in the group under study to that in a comparison group, with adjustment for confounding factors such as age, if necessary. For rare diseases the relative risk is similar to the odds ratio *(see above)*.

standardised mortality ratio (SMR)   the ratio of the observed number of deaths from a given cause in a cohort to that expected on the basis of both mortality rates for a general population and the age (and, if relevant, sex) distribution of person-years for the cohort. SMR is often expressed as a percentage, ie an SMR of 100 indicates that the age-adjusted mortality rate is the same in the cohort and the general population.